INTERPRETATION

OF THE

TAROT

Alena Seamore

Table of Contents

4

Introduction

In the sense of apology, I, Alena Seamore, believes that it seems more of necessity than predilection to record in the first place a plain statement of my personal position, as one who has been an exponent of the higher mystic schools for many years of my life, subject self to spiritual and other limitations. It's going to be thought that I'm acting strangely, apportioning about myself today with what appears within a glance and simply a well-known method of card reading and fortune-telling. However, the opinions of some fortune tellers, even in the literary reviews, are of no importance unless they agree with our own, but to sanctify this doctrine, we have to be careful that our opinions, and the subjects from which they arise, are concerned only with the highest ones.

Yet it is precisely this that, in the present instance, may seem doubtful, not only to those whom I respect within the proper measures of detachment but also to some more real consequence, seeing that their dedications are mine. To these and any, I would say that after the most enlightened Frater Christian Rosy Cross had beheld the Chemical

Marriage in the Transmutation Secret Palace, his story breaks abruptly, with an intimation that he expected to be doorkeeper next morning.

It happens more often than it might seem likely after the same manner that those who have seen the Occult Powers of Nature through the clearest veils of the sacraments are the ones who subsequently assume the humblest offices of all about the House of Wisdom. In the secret orders separated from the class of Neophytes as servi servorum mysterii are the Adepts and Great Masters also by these simple devices. So we also find the Tarot cards at the outermost door, or in a manner that is not quite unlike them, in the middle of the frittering and debris of the so-called magical arts, about which none in their senses has suffered the slightest deception. Yet, these cards are related to themselves in one area or the other, for they contain a very high meaning, understood according to the Laws of Grace.

The fact that God's wisdom (Nature) is foolishness with men does not create a presumption that this world's foolishness makes Divine Wisdom in any sense; therefore neither the scholars in the the lower classes nor the pedagogues in the seats of the High Priests and Lords will absolutely be quick and fast to sense the possibility or even the likelihood of this proposition. The subject was in the hands of cartomancists as part of their industry's stock-in-trade; I do not seek to persuade anyone outside of my own circles that this is of much or no consequence, but on the historical and interpretative sides it hasn't fared better; it has been in the hands of exponents. Those who have curated and brought it into utter contempt for those people who possess philosophy. It is time it was to be rescued, and I propose to undertake this once and for all, that I might have done with the side issues that distract from the term. Since poetry is the most beautiful expression of the things that are most beautiful of all, so is symbolism the most Catholic expression in the concealment of things that are most profound in the Sanctuary and that have not been declared with the same fullness by the spoken word outside it. The rationale of the law of silence is not part of my present interest, but I have put on record somewhere else, and quite recently, what can be said on this topic.

The little treatise that follows is divided into three sections, in the first of which I have dealt with the subject's antiquities and some issues that emerge from and interact with it.

It should also be of note that it is not put forward as a reference to the history of playing cards, of which I know nothing and care none; it is a thought devoted to and addressed to a certain school of occultism, especially in France, as to the root and core of all the phantasmagoria that has been articulated in the last 50 years under the pretext of considering Tarot, I dealt with the symbolism in the second part according to some of its higher and divine aspects. However, this also serves to introduce the complete and contemporary Tarot, which is available separately in the form of colored cards, the designs of which are added in black and white to the present text. Under my supervision, they were prepared — in terms of the attributions and meanings — by a lady who has high claims as an artist.

With regard to the divinatory part which is included in this book, I consider it a fact in the history of the Tarot; as such, from all the sources published, I have drawn a harmony of the meanings attached to the

13

various cards, and I have given prominence to one method of working which was not previously published; it has the merit of simplicity, while it is also unpublished.

Alena Seamore

PART I

THE VEIL AND ITS CARDS

Section 1

Welcome to Tarot Reading

In another world, the pathology the poet makes an expression that the undevout astronomer is mad; the very plain man's pathology says the genius is mad; and among these extremes, which stand for ten thousand analogous excesses, the sovereign reason takes a moderator's part and does what it can. I don't think there is a pathology of occult dedications. Still, no one can question their extravagances, and it's no less difficult than ungrateful to act as a moderator in their regard. Moreover, if it existed, the pathology would likely be empiricism rather than a diagnosis and would offer no criterion. Now occultism is not like mystical faculty, and it very rarely works in harmony either with business aptitude in the things of ordinary life or with knowledge of the evidence canons in its own sphere. I know that there are few things more dull for the high art of ribaldry than the criticism that maintains that a thesis is untrue and that it can not be understood as decorative. I also know that after a long time dealing with doubtful doctrine or with difficult research, it is always refreshing, in the realm of this art, to encounter what is obviously fraud or, at least, total unreason. Yet as seen through the prism of occultism, the facets of history are not, as a rule, beautiful and have few gifts of refreshment to heal the lacerations that they inflict upon the rational understanding. In the Rosy Cross Fellowship, it almost requires a Frater Sapiens dominabitur astris to have the patience that is not lost in the clouds of folly when the Tarot's consideration is undertaken in accordance with the higher law of symbolism. The true Tarot is symbolism; no other language is spoken, and no other signs are provided. Because of their emblems ' internal nature, they become a kind of alphabet that is capable of infinite combinations and makes real sense in all. It offers a "Key" to The Mysteries on the highest plane, in a manner that is not arbitrary and was not read in. But the wrong symbolic stories have been told about it, and in every published work that has dealt with the topic so far, the wrong history has been given. Two or three writers have intimated that this is undoubtedly the case, at least in terms of definitions, because few are familiar with them, while these few hang on to commitments through transmission and can not betray their faith. The suggestion on the surface is fantastic, as there appears to be some anti-climax in the proposition that a particular interpretation of fortune-telling— l'art de tirer les cartes — can be reserved for Sons of the Doctrine. Nonetheless, the fact remains that there is a Secret Tradition concerning the Tarot, and since there is always the possibility that some minor arcana of the Mysteries may be made public with a flourishing of trumpets, it will be wise to go before the event and inform those who are curious about such matters that any discovery may contain only one-third of the earth and sea and one-third of the earth and sea and a third part of the stars of heaven in respect of the symbolism. This is for the simple reason that more has not been written in either root-matter or development, so much will remain to be said after any pretended unveiling. Consequently, the guardians of certain initiation temples who keep watch over the mysteries of this order have no cause for alarm.

More precisely, as I have intimated, the present work is designed to introduce a rectified collection of the cards themselves and to tell the unadorned truth about them, as far as this is possible in the outer circles. As for the series of greater cards, their ultimate and supreme significance lies deeper than the typical picture or hieroglyphic language. Those who have received a part of the Secret Tradition will understand this. As for the verbal definitions given here to the more significant Trump Cards, they are intended to set aside the follies and impostures of past attributions, to place those who have the gift of wisdom on the right track, and to take care, within the limits of my possibilities, that they are the facts as far as they go.

It is regrettable that I must admit to certain reservations in several respects, but there is a question of honor at stake. Furthermore, among the follies on the first side of those who are quite ignorant of the practice, yet are, in their own view, the exponents of something called occult science and philosophy, and on the other, between the creeds of a few writers who have earned a part of the tradition and believe that it is a legitimate title to scatter dust in the eyes of the world without it.

In due course, we shall see that the history of Tarot cards is largely negative in nature, and that, when the issues are resolved by the dissipation of meditations and gratuitous speculations expressed in terms of certainty, there is, in fact, no history before the fourteenth century. The deceit and self-deception with regard to their roots in Egypt, India, or China brought a deceptive spirit into the mouths of the first expositors, and the later occult writers have done little more than repeating the first false testimony in good faith of an unwakened intellect to the research questions. As it happens, all exposures have worked within a very narrow range and owe little to the inventive faculty, in comparison. At least one great chance has been lost, as it has not happened to anyone so far that the Tarot may have made a task and even emerged as a hidden, language of the symbol of the Albigensian sects.

This suggestion is very recommended to the lineal descendants and other descendants in the spirit of Gabriele Rossetti and Eugène Aroux. And to Mr. Harold Bayley who is another member of the New Light On The Renaissance, and at least as a taper in the darkness which, with great respect, could be of service to Mrs. Cooper-Oakley's zealous and all-searching mind. Just think what the supposed testimony of watermarks on paper could gain from the Pope's or Hierophant's Tarot Card, in connection with the notion of a secret Albigensian patriarch, of whom Mr. Bayley found so much material for his purpose in these same watermarks. Think for a moment of the High Priestess ' card as representing the Albigensian church itself; and think of the Tower struck by Lightning as typifying the desired destruction of Papal Rome, the city on the seven hills, with the Pontiff and his temporal power cast down from the spiritual edifice when ripped away by the nature of the efficacies of God's wrath. The possibilities, however, are so numerous and persuasive that one of the elects who has invented them is almost deceived in their expression. But then, the fact remains that, there is more to it than this, although I never wish to quote it.

Also, when it was the exact time for the Tarot cards which are to be the subject of their first formal description, the archeologist Court de Gebelin replicated some of their most important emblems, and, if I may put it that way, the codex he used served as the source of reference for many subsequently published collections, by means of his engraved plates. The figures are very simple and, as such, vary from the cards of Etteilla, the Tarot of

Marseilles, and others still existing in some parts of France. It is important to be a good judge, which I may not be, but in such matters, but the fact that each of the Trump Major could have replied for watermark purposes is shown by the cases I have cited and by one of the most impressive examples of the Ace of Cups.

I should call it, in the manner of a ciborium, a Eucharistic emblem, but this does not mean at the moment. In the book, New Light On The Renaissance, Mr. Harold Bayley gives six similar devices as watermarks on seventeenth-century paper, which he claims to be of Albigensian origin, representing sacramental and Graal emblems.

Had he learned of the Tarot only, had he known that these cards of divination, cards of fortune, cards of all vagabond arts, were perhaps present in the South of France era, I think his enchanting but all too fantastic theory could have diluted even more in the atmosphere of his dreams. There is no doubt that we should have had a vision of Christian Gnosticism, Manichaeanism, and all that pure primitive Gospel he understands, shining behind the pictures.

21

I don't look through such glasses, and I can only commend the subject to his attention at a later stage; it's mentioned here that I can introduce the marvels of arbitrary speculation about the history of the cards with an unheard-of wonder.

Referring to their shape and number, it should hardly be necessary to list them, as they must be almost commonly known, but as it is precarious to assume anything, and as there are other reasons, I will briefly classify them as follows:-

CLASS I

Section 2

TRUMP MAJOR

OTHERWISE, GREATER ARCANA

1. In the world of vulgar trickery, the Magus, Magician, or Juggler, the caster of the dice and mountebank. This is the definition of colportage, and it has the same relationship with the true symbolic meaning that, according to the ancient science of magic, the Tarot's use in fortune-telling has with its magical creation. It must be added, however, that many independent students studying magic and tarot reading and fortune-telling have produced individual sequences of meaning to the Trump Major, following their own lights, and their lights are sometimes suggestive, but they are not the true lights. Eliphas Lévi, for example, says that the Magus signifies that unity, which is the mother of numbers; others say it is the Divine Unity, and one of the latest French commentators considers that it is the will in its general sense.

2. The High Priestess, Pope Joan, or Female Pontiff; early expositors sought to term this card as the Mother, or Pope's Wife, opposed to the symbolism. Occasionally it is considered to reflect the Divine Law and the Gnosis, in which case the Priestess refers to the Shekinah concept. She is, in essence, the Secret Tradition, and also the higher sense of the Mysteries being instituted.

3. The Princess, who is sometimes full-faced, while her contact, the Emperor, is in profile. Since there has been a tendency to attribute to this distinction a symbolic significance, it seems desirable to say that it has no inner meaning. The Empress was associated with the concepts of natural fertility, and with development in a general sense.

4. The Emperor, the former's spouse, by imputation. Aside from his insignia, he is occasionally represented as wearing the stars or ribbons of some order of chivalry. And in the bid to show and express that the cards are a medley of old and new emblems, I mention this. Those who rely on one's evidence should contend with the other if they can. No effective argument can be drawn from the fact that it incorporates old material for the antiquity of

a particular design. Still, there is also none that can be based on sporadic novelties, the intervention of which can only mean the unintelligent hand of an editor or a late draughtsman.

5. Also called the Spiritual Father is the High Priest or Hierophant, and more commonly and obviously the Pope. It even seems to have been called the Abbot, and then the Abbess or Mother of the Convent became his contact, the High Priestess. Both names are arbitrary. The symbol of the figures are papal, and in such a case, the High Priestess is and can be only the Church to whom the spiritual rite of ordination marries the Pope and priests. Nevertheless, I do believe that this card did not represent the Roman Pontiff in its primitive form.

6. Love or Matrimony. As expected from its subject, this symbol has undergone many variations. In the style of the eighteenth century, by which it first became known to the world of archeological science, it is really a card of married life, depicting father and mother, with their infant put between them; and, of course, the pagan Cupid above, in the act of flying his shaft, is a misused symbol. The Cupid, in his fullness, is of the beginning rather than of lust,

protecting the seed. The card is said to have been named Simulacrum Fidei, the emblem of conjugal fidelity for which the rainbow would have been a more fitting concomitant as a token of the covenant. The estimates are also considered to have represented Truth, Honour, and Respect, but I think this was the polish of a moralizing commentator. It has these, but there are other and greater dimensions to it.

7. The Wagon. In some current codices, this is depicted as being drawn by two sphinxes, and the system is in consonance with the symbolism, but it must not be believed that this was its original form; the variant was created to justify a specific historical interpretation. Black horses were yoked onto the automobile in the eighteenth century. As far as its usual name is concerned, the lesser stands for the greater; it is truly the King in his triumph, yet typifying the victory that creates kingship as its natural consequence and not the fourth card's vested royalty. M. Court de Gebelin said it was Osiris Triumphing, the spring-time rising light having overcome the winter obstacles. We now learn that Osiris is not portrayed by such simple cards as to rise from the dead. The currus triumphalis has also been

used to depict other animals besides horses, such as a lion and a leopard.

8. Fortune. This is one of the cardinal virtues which I will talk about later. In general, the female figure is represented as closing a lion's mouth. She is obviously opening it in the earlier form that Court de Gebelin prints. Symbolically, the first choice is stronger, but either is an indication of dominance in its modern sense, which conveys the concept of superiority. The figure has been said to represent organic strength, moral force, and the principle of all force.

9. The Hermit stands next on the list, as he is called in common parlance; he is also the Capuchin and the Sage in more philosophical language. He is said to be searching for the Truth that is in the sequence far away, and for the justice that preceded him on the way. But as we shall see later, this is an attainment card rather than a quest card. It is also said that his lamp contains Occult Science's Fire and that his belt is a Magic Staff. In every way, these definitions are equivalent to the divinatory and fortune-telling concepts I shall have to contend with in their turn. And in the end, we realize that the diabolism of both

instrument is that they are real according to their own way, but they skip all the high things to which the Greater Arcana should be entrusted. It is as though a man who knows in his heart that all roads lead to the heights and that God (Nature) is at the highest of all, should choose the path of perdition or the path of folly as the path of his own attainment. Eliphas Lévi assigned this card to Prudence, but in doing so, he was driven by the wish to fill a gap that would otherwise occur in the symbolism. For an ideological sequence like the Trump Major, the four cardinal virtues are necessary. Still, they must not be taken only in that first sense, which exists for the use and consolation of him who is called the man in the street in these days of halfpenny journalism. These are the correlatives of the counsels of justice in their proper understanding when they have been equally re-expressed, and they read as follows:

(A) Transcendental Truth, the counter-equilibrium of the scales, when they are over-weighted so that they fall strongly on God's (Nature) side. The appropriate counsel is to use the loaded dice when playing with Diabolus for high stakes. The axiom, aut nihil, is Aut Deus.

(B) Divine Ecstasy, which stand as a counterpoise to a fruit of the higher spirit called Temperance, which, I believe, is a sign of the extinction of the lights in the tavern. The related recommendation is to drink only new wine in the Father's Kingdom, for God (Nature) is in everything. The axiom is that man who is a rational being must become obsessed with God (Nature); Spinoza is the imputed case in point.

(C) The state of the Royal Fortitude of Supernatural Order, which is the state of the Tower of Ivory and of the House of Gold, but it is God (Nature) and not the man who became the Turris fortitudinis a facie inimici, and the enemy was cast out of that House. The corresponding advice is that even in the presence of death, a man must not spare himself, but he must be certain that his sacrifice will be the best—of any open course—to ensure his end. The axiom is that the strength that is elevated to such a degree that a man dares to lose himself will show him how Nature (God) is found, and thus dare and learn as to such refuge.

(D) Prudence is the economy that follows the least resistance path, so that the soul may return from whence it comes. It is actually a doctrine of absolute divine parsimony and energy conservation because of this life's stress, terror, and manifested impertinences. The corresponding counsel is that the one thing that is needed is true Prudence, and the axiom is: Waste not, they don't want. In conclusion, a business proposal based on the law of exchange: you can't help getting what you're looking for concerning Divine things: it's the law of supply and demand. I stated these few things at this stage for two simple reasons: (a) because the impartiality of the intellect, it sometimes seems more difficult to decide whether it is sin or vulgarity that pitifully ruins the present world; (b) because, to correct the imperfections of the old conceptions, it is sometimes quite important to use meaningless terms and phrases of the old notions.

10. The Wheel of Fortune. Wheel of Fortune. There is the current Manual of Cartomancy, which has gained considerable vogue in England and has intersected several serious subjects in a great dispersion of curious things. It deals with one aspect of the Tarot, and if I correctly interpret the author, this word is interpreted in my own context from beginning to end like a wheel of fortune. It exists throughout the world, and I wonder that it was not

previously taken as the most appropriate name in the common fate. It is also the title of one Trump Major, which, as my interpretation shows, is actually of our concern at the present time. In recent years, many fantastic presentations and a hypothetical reconstruction have suffered, which is evocative in its symbolism. The wheel contains seven radii; the ascending and descending animals were indeed non-described animals in the 18th century, one of them with a human head. The creature with the body of an infinite beast, wings on the shoulders, and a crown on the head were at the top. He held two walls between his hands. These are replaced by a Hermanubis with the wheel, a sphinx couchant at the summit, and a typhoon on the descending side during the reconstruction. Here is another example of an innovation to endorse a hypothesis; but if the latter is set aside, then the grouping is symbolically right and can go through.

11. Justice. That the Tarot is not of time immemorial, although it is of reasonable antiquity, is shown by the card which could have been presented in a far more archaic manner. However, those who have gifts of discernment in this way do not need to be told that age is in no way the essence of the consideration: in

the third craft level of masonry, the rite of closing the Lodge may be from the late 18th century, but it does not signify anything. The female character of the 11th card is said to be Astræa, who reflected the same virtue and symbolized the same. Despite this goddess and despite the vulgar Cupid, the Tarot is not of the Roman mythology or of Greek either. His presentation of Justice was to be one of the four cardinal virtues contained in the sequence of Greater Arcana. Still, the fourth emblem was desired, and the commentators had to discover it at any cost. They did what they could and still study laws that have never managed to remove the missing Persephone by being prudent. Court de Gebelin tried by a tour de force to resolve the difficulty by believing that he had extracted from the Hanged Man's symbol what he wanted—from which he deceived himself. The Tarot, therefore, has its Justice and its power, but because of a peculiar omission, it offers us no prudence. However, it can be accepted that, in some respects, the solitude of the hermit, following an isolated course in the light of its own lamp, gives a certain high counsel for those who can obtain it with regard to the Via Prudentia.

12. The Hanged Man. That is the sign this Prudence is to represent, and Eliphas Lévi states, in his shallowest and most logical way, that he is an adept bound by his obligations. A man's figure is hung head-down from a gibbet, to which he is bound with a rope about one of his ankles. Behind him are the arms bound, and one leg is crossed over. According to another, and indeed to the current interpretation, it means sacrifice, but the intuitions of Cartaomancists, in addition to any real value, on the symbolic side are all current values assigned to this coin. The eighteenth-century fortune-tellers, who embraced Tarot, showed a semi-feminine youth in jerkin, which was standing on one foot loosely attached to a short stake, which was driven into the ground.

13. Life. The presentation method is almost unchanging and embodies a bourgeois symbolism. The scene is a field of life, and there are living arms and heads from the ground in the midst of ordinary rank vegetation. One of the heads is crowned, and it is pushed by a skeleton with a large scythe. The straightforward and inevitable definition is death, but transition and transformation are the alternatives allocated to the sign. Other heads were previously swept from their place, but it is more

particularly a card of Kings ' death in its current and patent meaning. In the exotic sense, the ascent of the spirit in the divine spheres, creation and destruction, perpetual movement, and so on have been said to mean.

14. Temperance. The winged figure of a female who is normally allocated to this order of ministering spirits, in contrast to all doctrines concerning the hierarchy of the angels, is poured liquid from pitcher to pitcher. Dr. Papus leaves the traditional form in his last work on the Tarot and portrays a woman wearing an Egyptian headdress. The first thing that appears clear on the surface is that the whole symbol has no special relation to temperance, and the fact that this card designation has always been obtained offers a clear indication of meaning, namely the title in chief for the Tarot as a whole.

15. The devil. This card appeared to be a symbol of pure animal impudicity in the eighteenth century. The leading figure is completely naked except for a beautiful headdress, and it has bat-like wings and hands and feet portrayed by the claws of an eagle. In the right hand is a wand ending in a symbol that is supposed to represent a spark. The figure as a whole is not especially evil; it has no tail, and the

commentators have spoken loosely about the paws. The alternative suggestion that they are the eagle's claws is no better ground. Two small demons, probably male and female, are connected by a cord depending on their heads to the pedestal on which the figure is placed. These are tailed, but they are not winged. Since 1856, the effect of Eliphas Lévi and his occult doctrine has changed the face of this card, and now appears as a Pseudo-Baphomet figure with the head of a goat and the big flares between the horns, and is sitting instead of straight. There is the Hermetic caduceus instead of generative organs. In the Tarot Divinatory of Papu, the little ghosts, both male and female, are replaced by naked human beings who are yoked together. This improved symbolism can be congratulated to the poet.

16. Lightning struck the Tower. Its other names are Plutus Castle, God's House, and Babel Tower. In the latter case, Nimrod and his minister are the figures falling from it. Certainly, it is a confusing card, and in general, it corresponds to any of the designations except the House of God, except when we understand that the House of God (Nature) is left and the veil of the temple is rented. It is somewhat surprising that the device has not yet been

designated to destroy the Temple of Solomon when the lightning symbolizes the fire and sword by which the King of the Chaldees visited the building.

17. The Star, Dog-Star, or Sirius, also called the star of the Magi fantastically. Seven little luminaries are grouped around her, and underneath is a naked female figure with her left knee on the ground and her right foot on the water. She's in the act of pouring two vessels of fluids out. A bird is placed on a tree near her; in some future cards, a butterfly on a rose was replaced by this. So the Star was also called Hope. This is one of the cards that Court de Gebelin describes as being entirely Egyptian — in his meditation.

18. The Moon. The Moon. Some cards from the 18th century show the luminary on its diminutive side; in Etteilla's degraded edition, it is the moon in fullness in the nights, placed in starry heaven; in recent years, the moon is shown on the side of its increase. In almost every lecture, she shines brightly and moisturizes the fertilizing dew with big drops. Below are two buildings, which wind a path to the horizon's edge. Two dogs, or wolf and dog, bay at the moon,

and there is water in the foreground which moves to the land a crayfish.

19. The Sun. The Sun. The luminary is characterized by primary tossed, salient, and salient secondary rays in older cards. This tends to affect the earth not only through light and heat but also—like the moon—by drops of dew. Court of Gebelin called those gold and pearl tears, just as the lunar dew was identified with the Isis tears. Underneath the dog star, there is a wall that reflects the walled garden—as it could be, a wall—in which two children face a stream, gambling or running hand in hand, either nude or loosely dressed. Eliphas Lévi says that sometimes they are replaced by a spinner-free destiny and another far better symbol— the naked children mounted on a white horse and standard scarlet.

20. The last decision. The last verdict. I have already talked about this symbol, whose form is essentially unchanging, even in the Etteilla set. The angel plays his trumpet in the area of the cemetery, and the dead awaken. No matter, Etteilla omits the fairy, or that Dr. Papus substitutes a ridiculous figure, but in line with the general intent of the set Tarot that follows his latest work. We should feel very

confident about our ground before rejecting the transparent interpretation of the symbolism transmitted by the names of the card and the picture it presents to the eye. It is and can only be the resurrection on the surface of this triad—the father, mother, and child—which we met in the eighth card. M. Bourgeat risks suggesting that it is esoterically the symbol of evolution— of which there are no signs. The Court de Gebelin is unlikely as normal and pointed out that when gravel pierces were removed, and it might be recognized as a sign of creation. Some claim that it implies rebirth, which is clear enough; that it is the triad of human life; that it is the "generative force of the world... and of eternal life."

21. The Fool, which is mostly a cipher card, but is nothing numbers— the Fool, Mate, or Unwise Man. Court de Gebelin sets it as the zero or negative at the head of the entire series, pre-assumed by numeration, and as this is simple, it is also a better arrangement. It was discarded as later the cards were assigned to the Hebrew alphabet letters and there were issues with the classification of the zero cards in a series of letters, which all represent numbers. In the current reference to the letter Shin,

which is 200, the difficulty or unreason remains. The reality is that the cards have never really been set. The Fool holds a bag; he looks over his shoulder and doesn't know he's on the bottom of a steep slope, but a dog or other beast is attacking him — others call it tiger — and he's rushing to his demise. Etteilla gave this piece, as it is commonly understood, a justifiable variant in the shape of a court jester with the hat, bells, and sugar. The other descriptions state that the wallet contains the insanities and vices of the bearer, which appear bourgeois and arbitrary.

22. The world, the world or the world, or time. The four living beings of Revelation and Ezekiel's dream, which the evangelists referred to in Christian mythology, are clustered around an elliptical garland as if it were a chain of flowers intended to represent all things sensitive; within this garland is a lady, with a light scarf about her loins and all her vesture. She's spinning, and she has a wall on both sides. It is an eloquent illustration of the whirlwind of delicate creation, of the flesh ecstasy, of the madness of the spirit in earthly Paradise, but still guarded by the Divine Watchers, as if by the Holy Name's forces and graces Tetragrammaton, the four ineffable letters that are often credited to the mysterious beasts.

Eliphas Lévi calls a crown the garland and reports the facts. Dr. Papus relates it to the Universal and to the knowledge of the Grand Work; for other aspects, it is a sign of nature and an everlasting reward for a good life. In the four quarters of the insurgency, four flowers are clearly identified. Following the concepts created by P. Christian, the guerrilla should be formed of roses, and that is the kind of chain that is less easily broken by Eliphas Lévi than the chains of iron. And perhaps by antithesis, but in alligeience with same reason, Peter's iron crown can lie louder on sovereign papal heads than the golden crown on Kings.

CLASS II

Section 3

THE FOUR SUITS

OTHERWISE, LESSER ARCANA

The interpretive resources on the 22 Trump Major, which are symbolically unquestionable, were prolific, if not exhausted.

The four suits remained:
Wands — former theory, the predecessor to the Diamonds in modern cards in the archaeology of the subject.
Cups corresponding to Hearts.
Swords which respond to Clubs, since chivalric arms are related to the quarter personnel of the peasants or the Alsatian bloodgeon.
The Pentacles— also called Deniers or Dollars — which are the variants of Spades. There are 10 numbered cards for old as in new suits, but in Tarot, four court cards are allocated, or one Knight is allotted, in addition to King, Queen, and Knave. The Knave is a page, a valet, or a damoiseau; most

correctly, it is an esquire, probably at the service of a ruler, but some rare sets are in place in which the page becomes an honorary maid, pairing the sexes with the cards on the tetrad. There is, of course, a characteristic branding of the various pictures, which indicates that the king of walls is not exactly the same person as the king of cups, even after the numerous emblems they carry have been granted. Still, the significance remains in their rank and their uniform. Also, the smaller cards, which have never been issued in pictures in these modern days until now, depending on the specific significance of the particular suit in connection with their numbers. Therefore, before I come to talk in the second part of the Tarot, which accompanies this work, I reserve the specifics of Lesser Arcana. The third part is the plurality of divinatory interpretations added to the greater and lesser cards.

Section 4

HISTORY OF TAROT

Our next immediate concern is to talk about the history of tarot cards in order to dispose of once and for all of the speculations and stereotypes perpetuated and multiplied in occult research schools, as explained in the preface.

At the beginning of this point, let us understand that there are several sets or sequences of ancient cards that are part of our concern. The Tarot Of The Bohemians from Papus, which I recently went through the papers, which checked the flawed version, has some useful information in this respect and is intended for the general reader except for the lack of dates and other evidence of the historical context. I am not proposing to extend this in any way, which can be called significant, but certain additions are desirable and thus a distinct way of presentation.

Among the ancient cards mentioned in connection with Tarot, there are first of all those of Baldini, the celebrated set attributed to Andrea Mantegna by tradition. However, this view is currently generally refused. Their date should be around 1470, and only four specimens are known to survive in Europe. Perhaps a copy or reproduction referred to in 1485 is just as rare. A complete set contains 50 numbers divided into 5 denarii or 10 card sequences. There seems to be no evidence that they were used for any game, whether of chance or of competence; they could hardly have devoted themselves to religion, or to any sort of fortune-telling; though it is more than idle to associate their apparent emblematic designs with a profound symbolic meaning. The first denary contains the terms of life: (1) the Beggar, (2) the Knave, (4) the Merchant, (5) the Noble, (6) the King, (7) the Doge, (8) the King, (9) the Emperor and (9) the Pape. The first denarius is the Conditions of life, as follows: The second contains: (11) Calliope, (12) Uranian, (13) Terpsichore, (14) Erato, (15) Polyhymnian, (16) Thalia, (17) Thalia, (17), (18) Euterpe, (19) Clio, (20) Apollo. The second contains: The third one brings together a part of liberal arts and sciences with other human learning departments as follows: (21) Grammar, (22) Logic, (23) Rhetoric, (24) Geometric, (25) Arithmetic, (26) Music, (27) Poetry, (28) Astrology, (30) Theology. The fourth denaire ends the Liberal Arts and lists the virtues: (31) Astronomy, (32) Chronology, (33) Cardiovascular, (34) Temperance, (35) Prudence,

(37) Justice, (38) Charity, (39) Hope, (40) Faith. The fifth and final denarius presents the system of the Heavens: (41) Moon, (42) Mercury, (43) Venus, (44) Sun, (45) Mars, (47) Jupiter, (48) Saturn, (49).

We must set aside fantastic attempts at extracting the entire Tarot sequence from these denarii; we must, for example, forbear from saying that the Life Conditions are consistent with the Major Trumps, the Pentacle Muses, the Cups, the Virtues, etc., wands, and the living conditions of Swords. A mental distortion process can do this kind of thing, but in reality, it has no place. At the same time, in the same period of years, it is difficult for each card to display clear, even shocking, analogies. The Baldini King, Knight, and Knave propose Minor Arcana's corresponding court cards. The Mantagna and Trump Major of any Tarot pack are the Emperor, the Pope, Temperance, Strength, Justice, Moon, and Sun. Predisposition has also connected Beggar and Fool with the Star, with Venus and Star, with Mars and Chariot, with Saturn and Hermit, and also with Jupiter or the First Cause with the world Tarot. And the Trump Major main features are desirable in the Mantegna set, and I don't think the order in the latter case gave birth, as suggested, to that Trump Major, Romain Merlin maintained this view and at the end of the fourteenth century positively assigned Baldini symbols.

If it is agreed that the emblematic or allegorical pictures of the Baldini have a mysterious and rare connection with the Tarot cards, even briefly and sporadically, and that they can not provide any originating intent, it follows that we are still searching not only for a reference in place and time for the cards with which we are concerned but for the particular case. We now know that in 1393 the painter Charles Gringonneur, who was not named an Occultist and Kabalist by an indifferent English writer for no reason whatsoever traceable, was creating and illuminating certain types of cards for the diversion of Charles VI of France when he was mentally ill and whether he could establish anything. The only reason is that 17 cards are drawn and illuminated on paper in Paris, in the Bibliothèque du Roi. They are very elegant, vintage, and unpriced; the figures have a gold background and are set in metal, but no inscription and numbers are added.

However, it is certain that they include Tarot Trump Major, the following list of which are: Fool, Emperor, Pape, Lovers, Wheel of Fortune, Temperance, Fortune, Justice, Moon, Sun, Chariot, Ermita,

Hanged Man, Death, Tower, and Last Judgement. Four tarot cards are also available at the Musée Carrer, Venice, and five elsewhere. It contains two pages or Knaves, three Kings, and two Queens, illustrating the Arcana Minor. These collections have all been identified by the set produced by Gringonneur, but the claim has been disputed until 1848 and is apparently not presented today, even by those who want to make the ancient Tarot evident. They are all of the Italian origin and some of the Venetian origin, at least. In this way, we have at least our required point of departure for the place. It has also been said that the Venetian Tarots are the old and true form, the parent of all others; but I conclude that the entire Arcane of the Mayors and the Minors belongs to much later periods. The box is expected to consist of 78 cards.

However, it is recognized that some portions of the Minchiate or Florentine set have to be allocated to the period between 1413 and 1418, despite the preference shown for the Venetian Tarot. Once, they were owned by Countess Gonzaga in Milan. A full Minchiate pack included 97 cards and is considered a later invention that was given to these vestiges. There were 41 Major Trumps, and the additional numbers were borrowed or reflected in the emblematic set of Baldini. The knights were centaur-type creatures in the court cards of the Minor Arcana, whereas the knaves were sometimes guerrillas and servicemen. The prevalence of medieval Christian ideas and the complete absence of any Oriental suggestion are also a distinction. The question remains, however, whether any Tarot card has Eastern traces.

In good, we come to the Bolognese Tarot, also called Venice, and complete the Trump Major, but the numbers 20 and 21 are transposed. The 2, 3, 4, and 5 minor cards in the Minor Arcana are omitted, resulting in 62 cards in all. The termination of the Trump Major in the depiction of the Last Judgement is curious, and it is a little bit more arresting as an illustration, but this is all it seems appropriate to comment about the Bologna deck except that it has, as a Tarot, been invented— or, more accurately, changed— by the exiled prince of Pisa living in the city about the beginning of the 15th century. The use they found tolerable was made clear by the fact that St. Bernardine of Siena protested in 1423 against playing cards and other gaming types. Forty years later, it was prohibited to import cards to England, at this time the import to King Edward IV. This is the first record in our country of the subject.

Perfect examples of the above collections are very difficult to obtain, but it is not difficult to find detailed and outlined descriptions — I would note, given that the author is not an occultist since the origins of accounts are generally incomplete, ambiguous, and worried with concerns clouding critical issues. Some views that have been expressed about the Mantegna codex give an example — if I can continue to dignify card sequences with such a title. As we have seen, in occult reservations, it has been rejected that Apollo and the Nine Muses correspond with Pentacles, but the analogy is not working in a research stage; and meditation must border on nightmare before we can identify Astronomy, Chronology, and Cosmology in a Cup suit. The Baldini characters that these subjects depict are emblems of their days rather than cards, like the Tarot.

In addition, I note that analysts were willing to believe that the Trump Major was not initially connected to the numbered suits. I would not offer a personal view; I am not an expert in the history of games of chance, and I do not like the profanum vulgus of divinatory cards. But I am keen in every respect to intimate that, if late research justifies such a decline, so much will be better for Greater Arcana, except for the good old art of telling fortune and its tamperings with so-called fate.

As far as what is necessary for the preliminary aspects of the historical aspects of Tarot cards is concerned, I shall now take up the speculative side of the subject and test its value. In my preface to The explicit Tarot Of bohemians, I said that the first author to make the facts known was the archeologist Court de Gebelin, who had spent several years in his Monde Primitif publication, which spanned nine fourth volumes just before the French Revolution. He was a learned man from his era, a high-grade mason, a member of the historical Philalethes lodge, and a virtuoso who was profoundly and lifelong interested in debating universal antiques before the science of the topic existed. His memorials, history and dissertations, collected under the title I mentioned, are worthwhile even today.

By the accident of things, when it was completely unknown in Paris, he got to know the Tarot and immediately thought it to be the remains of an Egyptian book. He made inquiries and discovered

50

that a significant portion of Europe — Spain, Italy, Germany and the South of France — is in transit. It was used in the normal way as a game of chance or skill; he discovered further how the game was played. But it was also used for the higher purpose of divination or good fortune, and with the aid of an accomplished friend he figured out the value of cards and the system adopted for this purpose. In brief, he has made a clear contribution to our knowledge and remains a reference source, but it is only on the matter of fact, and not on the cherished idea that the Tarot comprises mere Egyptian theory. He nevertheless expressed the opinion which remains prevalent in occult schools to this day, that the origin of the cards was lost in mystery and wonder, the weird night of the gods, the unknown language and the undeciphered hieroglyphs that symbolized Egypt at the end of the XVIIIth century.

This is how one of the characteristic literati of France dreamed, and it is almost understandable and sympathetic than the country about the Delta and the Nile began to be concerned for learning thinking, and the omne ignorum pro omnipresent was how many minds deluded themselves. It was excusable enough at that time, but that madness persisted and still spreads from mouth to mouth in the charming world of magical sciences— there is no reason for that. Therefore, let us see the evidence produced by M. Court de Gebelin, in support of his thesis, and to be fair to me, shall summarize it in his own words to the greatest extent possible.

The allegories are in keeping with the political, theological and religious teachings of ancient Egypt; (3) if the cards were new, there would be no high priestess included among the great Arcanes; (4) the person at issue would bear the horns of Isis; (5) the card called Emperor has a wand that ends on the road.

That is the evidence since I have set aside some informal remarks for which there is no excuse. These, therefore, are ten pillars that sustain the thesis building, and these are sand pillars. Of example, the Tarot is allegorical — that is, symbolism — but it is all-Catholic allegory and symbol— from all cultures, societies and times; they're Egyptian too, they're Asia and Cathay, Tibet beyond the Himalayas, London gutters. As an allegory and emblem, the cards suit a variety of ideas and things; common and not particular; and it is evident from the loss of the court of Gebelin, that they do not particularly and peculiarly respond to Egyptian philosophy, whether theological, metaphysical or political. The awesomeness and presence of a spiritual high priestess among the Trump Major can be clarified more simply as the commemoration of a common superstition— this worship of Diana, for example, whose existence is traced by Leland in modern Italy. In every cult, we must also remember the universality of the horns, not excluding Tibet. The Triple Cross, as an example of Egyptian symbolism, is absurd; both Greek and Latin—of Venice and Jerusalem, for instance—are the cross of the Patriarchal See and the form of signing used to this day by the priests and the laity of the Orthodox rite. In the case of a seventeenth card, it's a Sirius star or the other as a predisposition pleases; the number seven was surely important in Egypt and all the numerical mystical treatises will show that the same statements apply everywhere even if we choose to ignore the seven Chris I'm not aware that they are Hebrew Jods. Conclusively, regarding the etymology and origination of the word,Tarot, it is enough to note that before the finding of the Rosetta Steine it was offered long before the Egyptian language became known.

Court de Gebelin's work did not sit unnoticed in the mind of history, speaking solely to the learned through a quarter of a volume. It created the chance of the Tarot cards in Paris as the center of France and all French things in the universe. The suggestion that divination by cards was accompanied by the unexpected warrants of ancient hidden science, that the root of the entire subject was in the wonder and mystery of Egypt, reflects almost a divine dignity. Cartomancy emerged from the purlieus of occult practices and virtually at the moment assumed pontifical vestments. One person, who played the role of bateler, magician and juggler, was Aliette, an illiterate but zealous adventurer. The second, as a type of high priestess, was Miss. Lenormand — but she belongs to a later period; Julia Orsini finally came here, who refers to a Cup Queen in the tatters of light. I don't deal with those people as wealthy men, when fate was shuffling and cards for the universal revolutionary game or for courts and brokers such as Louis XVIII, Carlos IX, and Louis Philippe. But under the occult name of Andteilla, the transliteration of his name, Alliette, that perruquier was more severe than an ordinary fan in l'art de tirer les cartes and was a priest of the occult sciences. Even today, people, like Dr. Papus, tried to save some part of his odd system from forgetfulness.

The ancient story of Le Monde Primitif had ended in 1782, and Etteilla tracts had begun to be published in 1783, showing that he had already spent almost 40 years studying Egyptian magic and found the final keys. In truth, they were the core of the Tarot, which was a book of religion and a book of Thoth. At the same time, though, seventeen Magi composed it in a Temple of Fire, on the frontier of the Levant, around three Memphi leagues. This included the sciences of the cosmos and, without any hesitation or any restriction whatsoever, the cartomancist extended it to Astrology, Alchemy, and Fortune-telling. I have little doubt that he found this to be true as a career, and that he himself was the first one he was persuaded of his method. But the point we have to note is that the antiquity of the Tarot was so generally trumpeting. The small books of Etteilla are positive proof that he did not even know his own language. Even those who tenderly admit that he spoiled its emblem in time produced a reformed tarot, and in antiquities, only Court de Gebelin was his universal authority.

The Cartomancists followed each other, as I said, and, undoubtedly, rival adherents of these less than the least mysteries; but if the topic was said to exist, it was still more than sixty years in the quarter of Court de Gebelin. There is very little doubt about its power that everyone who, by theory or practice, by casual or special concern, has become acquainted with the question of Tarot cards has accepted its Egyptian character. Things are said to be taken as a matter of course because — according to the line of least resistance — the undesirable general mind recognizes historical pretensions in the sense of their own audacity and of those who support them. The first person who seemed to reconsider this subject with presumptive titles to a hearing was the French author Duchesne. Still, I have to pass on a simple reference and, therefore, some interesting studies on the general subject of Singer's play cards in England. The latter claimed that the ancient Venetian game Trappola was the first European card player, that it was of Arab origin, and that the fifty-two cards that were used for that reason originated in the region. I don't know that this perspective has ever been assigned any value.

Another English writer, W, followed Duchesne and Singer. A. Chatto, who studied the reality of this topic and the storm of speculations already emerging. That was in 1848, and his work still has a kind of standard authority, but after all allowances for a certain justice attributable to the independent mind, his performance remains indifferent and even poor. Nevertheless, it was typical of the midnight approaching of the 19th century. Chatto rejects the Egyptian hypothesis, but because he is struggling very quickly, he would hardly displace the Court de Gebelin if it had any solid foundation under his hypothesis. In 1854, another French scholar, Boiteau, took up the general issue and retained, without trying to prove it, the oriental roots of Tarot cards. I don't know, but I think he's the first writer to identify them definitely with the Gipsies; however, for him, the original Gipsy home was in India, and therefore Egypt didn't enter his calculation.

In 1860, the brilliant and deeply illuminated Eliphas Lévi came up, whom we can not accept and with whom we can dispense even more. There never was a mouth that announced such great things from all the western traditions that proclaimed or interpreted science as the supernatural and mystical doctrine. I suppose he cared profoundly for the phenomenal aspect, but he clarified the phenomenon with the confidence of someone who freely viewed charlatanism as a fantastic means to an end if it was used in a right cause. He came to his own and got him, even on his own behalf, as a man of great intelligence—never to have been –and as a revelator, without possessing any, of all mysteries. I do not believe there has ever been an example of a writer with greater gifts after their own kind who put them into such indifferentkind of usage. In the end, however, he was only Etteilla a second time in his flesh, with a mouth of gold and wider casual knowledge in his transmutation.

Nevertheless, he wrote the most complete, beautiful, enchanting history of magic ever published in any language. The Tarot and the theory of De Gebelin, taken into his hands, and all of mystical France and all of mystic Britain, Martinists, partially learned kabalists, schools of soi-disant theosophy— here and all over the world — have embraced his opinion with the same faith as his readings of these great kabal myths, which he had yelled and not taught. The Tarot was not only for him the perfect divinations instrument and keystone of occult science; it was also the primitive book, the only book by the ancient wise men, the miraculous volume that inspired all the sacred writings of ancient times. In his first work, however, Lévi was pleased to accept the construction of the Court of Gebelin and to repeat the seventh Trump Major with some Egyptian features. Tarot's transmission via the Gipsies did not take him until J. In his work on these wandering tribes, A. Vaillant, a bizarre writer with great knowledge of the Roman people, suggested it. The two writers clashed almost and then mirrored one another. It remained with the Roman Merlin, in 1869, to show what ought to have been clear, namely that a sort of game was recognized in Europe before the Gipsies arrived in or about 1417. But since this has been their arrival in Lüneburg and their presence can be traced back to earlier times, a considerable part of their influence has been lost to the correction. It is, therefore, safer to say that no reason was proposed for the Romany tribes ' use of the Tarot until after 1840;

We have now seen no evidence of the Egyptian origin of Tarot cards. Moving in other ways, cards of some kind were once invented in China around the year A. D. 1120. 1120. Court de Gebelin trusted in his passion for having traced them to a Chinese inscription of great ancient times, which is said to be relating to the subsidence of the waters of the Deluge. The characters of this inscription were in 77 compartments, and this makes up the analogy. India also had its tablets, whether cards or not, and these suggested similar slim similarities. But the evidence of certain existence, for instance, of ten suits or styles, each with a number of twelve, depicting the avatars of Vishnu such as fish, tortoise, boar, lion, monkey, hatchet, umbrella or bow, like a goat and a sheep and a fine horse, will not help us towards the origins of Trump Major or the presence of Crowns and Harps — or the presence of potential monkeys as a synonym for deniers and perhaps even harps. It would be fascinating if every language, man, environment, and time had its cards, and they were metaphysical, religious, and gambled, but unless they were Tarot cards, they would demonstrate man's inherent tendency to follow the same thing more or less fairly.

I, therefore, end the history of this topic, repeating that before the 14th century, when the first card rumors were heard, there was no history. They may have been around for centuries, but this would be early enough if people only intended to try their luck at playing or luck in seeing the future; on the other hand, if they have the secret doctrinal intimations, then the 14th century will return early enough or at least in this sense, we will get as much as we can.

PART II

THE DOCTRINE BEHIND THE VEIL

Section 1

THE TAROT AND SECRET TRADITION

The Tarot encompasses symbolic presentations of universal ideas, which have the whole implications of the human mind. In that sense, they contain a secret doctrine which, however, has not been explicitly acknowledged in ordinary people by the few truths imbued with the conscious. The hypothesis is that this ideology has always been present— that is, that it has been engrossed in the mind of a chosen minority; that it has been perpetuated from one human to the next in the underground, such as Alchemy and Kabalist literature; that it is also found in those established mysteries of which Rosicrucianism has set an example in the past, close to our ears. To solidify claims, it is very evident that there is an experience or practice behind the secret doctrine by which the doctrine is justified. It is evident that I can do little more than state the arguments in a textbook such as the present one, which, however, have been thoroughly addressed in several other documents, while it is designed to treat two of its most important processes in the books on the Hidden Religion of Freemasonry and Hermetic Literature.

About the claims made by Tarot, we must not neglect that a considerable portion of the Hidden Doctrine is portrayed in the pictorial emblems of the Alchemy so that the Book Of Thoth imputed is by no means a singular instrument of this emblematic sort. Alchemy now has two branches, as I have explained elsewhere, and both divisions share the pictorial emblems I mentioned. His material face is represented by the strange symbolism of the Mutus Liber, printed in Mangetus's great folios. The process of the great transmutation work is represented here in 14 copper-plate gravures, which display the various stages of the matter in the various chemical vessels. Above these vessels are mythological, planetary, solar, and lunar cards, like the powers and virtues which, according to Hermetic teaching, have been actively involved in the development and perfection of the metallic kingdom in helping the two operators who work below. Curiously enough, the workers are both male and female. The spiritual side of Alchemy resides in the far stranger emblems of the Lambspring Book, and I have already provided a partial explanation of it, which the reader may relate to2. The tract includes the mystery of what is called the supernatural or arch-natural elixir, the union of the mind and of the spirit within the philosopher's body and transmutation of the bo I've never met more curious intimations than in this small work. It is a fact that both tracts are much later than the last date that can be assigned by drastic criticism to the general distribution of Tarot cards in Europe. They belong to the end of the 17th and 16th centuries, respectively. Since I am not relying upon the imagination in order to recreate reality and knowledge, I do not say that the Tarot set the example of Hidden Doctrine in the picture and that Hermetic authors preceded it, but it is evident that it is perhaps the first example of this craft. It is also more catholic as, by definition or otherwise, it is not taken from any academy or literature of occultism; it is not from alchemy or kabalism nor from astrology or ritual magic; but, as I said, it is the introduction of abstract thoughts by means of universal forms, which it is expressed in the combination of these types, if any, with Secret Doctrine.

This combination may, for example, lie in the numerical sequence of its series, or its fortuitous assembly by shuffling, cutting, and handling, as in the ordinary luck games played with cards. Two scholars have taken the first opinion without bias to the second, and I may do well to determine what they mean at once. Mr. MacGregor Mathers, who once wrote a book about the Tarot, which was primarily dedicated to fortune-telling, stated that according to their numerical order, the twenty-two Trump Major could be formed as a' linked sequence.' It was indeed the chiefs of the philosophical theory on human will, the liberation by reason, which the magician embodied, its manifestation. He always spoke about prudence, determination, commitment, hope, and eventual satisfaction in the usual way. But if this were the message from the coins, there is no need at all to publish them today or take pains to explain them for some time. In his Tarot Of The Bohemians, a work written with passion and zeal wasted no effort to think or to study in its specific directions— but unfortunately without any true insight — Dr. Papus gave the Trump Major a singularly elaborate scheme. Like Mr. Mathers, it depends on their numeric sequence but shows their interrelationship in the Divine World, the Macrocosm and the Microcosm. In this way, we see, as it were, the metaphysical part of the man or of the soul coming out of the Divine, going back to the darkness of the material body. I believe that the author is in a measurable distance from the right track here, and his views are in this way informational, but in some ways, his method confuses the issues and modes and planes of being.

Trump Major was handled in the alternative way I described. In Grand Orient's Manual Of cartomancy, the product of certain illustrative readings of cards was actually organized as a result of a fortuitous combination by mixing and sorting under the assumption of a style of intuitive divination. The use of divinatory techniques, for any reason or intention, holds two ideas. It can be assumed that the deeper significance is not real, but that certain cards, such as the Magician, the High Priestess, the Wheel of Fortune, the Hanged Man, the Tower or House God, and many others, that do not correspond to life conditions, arts, sciences, virtues or the other subjects in Baldini's denarius, are not real. These are also positive evidence that the series can not be explained by simple and normal values. These cards testify to themselves in another manner, and, although the condition in which I left the Tarot is so much more difficult as it is so much more open, they indicate the real subject matter we deal with. The methods also show that the Trump Major has at least been adapted instead of belonging to fortune-telling. The may divinatory meanings that are given in the third part are largely arbitrary attributions or the result of secondary, uninitiated intuition, or they belong to the subject, apart from the original intention, at the most on a lower plane. If the Tarot was to say goodbye in his root matter, we should look for the motive for Witchcraft and the Black Sabbath in very weird places rather than any secret teaching.

Both the two meaning classes that are attached to the Tarot in the higher and lower worlds and the fact that no occult or other writer has sought to attribute anything but a divinatory meaning to Minor Arcana justify the hypothesis that the two series are not one to the other. It is possible that their marriage was first carried out by the Prince of Pisa in the Tarot of Bologna, whom I mentioned in the first part. It is said that his device has been given the public recognition and reward of his city of adoption for producing a tarot which has missed just a few cards in these fantastic days, but since we are dealing with a matter of fact that has to be taken into account somehow, it is conceivable that a sensation may have been created through It would have been more applied to the other chance game, known as fortune-telling. It should be understood here that I do not deny the option of divination, but as mystical of the dedications that bring people in these paths, I take exception as if they were linked with the mystical quest.

The Tarot cards issued by Miss Pamela Colman Smith in the little edition of the present work, i.e. the key to the tarot, were designed and colored, and will, I think, be very striking and beautiful in design and execution. They are reproduced as a reference to the text in the present enlarged edition of the Key. In many respects they differ from the traditional archaisms of the past and the miserable colportage products that now come from Italy, and I have to justify their variations as regards symbolism. That in modern times I present an artist's package for once does not demand apology, I presume, even to those people—when there are any of us—who were described before and call themselves "very obscene." If anybody looks at the beautiful Tarot valet or knave that is emblazoned on one of Chatto's page plates and speculation on the history of play cards, I could only hope that the restored and rectified card could be issued to the same extent and style; the designs would have been fairer to such a course, but for those practical purposes which are connected with a card and which allowance must be given, regardless of my views, the result would not have been manageable. I am solely responsible for the changes in the terminology by which compositions have been influenced. They would certainly attack scholars, real and imputed, on Major Arcana. I want to say therefore, within the reserves of courtesy and the convenience of the research fellowship, that I care not entirely for any opinion that may find expression. There is a Secret Tarot tradition as well as a Secret Doctrine contained therein; I have followed some of it without going beyond the bounds drawn by this kind of subject and belongs to the laws of honor. There are two parts of this practice and since one of them is written it seems that at any moment it may be deceived, which does not mean, because the other, as I have mentioned, is still less so and is owned by very few. The suppliers of fake copies and traffickers in stolen goods may, if they so wish, take notice of this. I also ask, in recent times, to distinguish between two or three authors, who thought they were fit to point out that they could say much more, if they liked it, because we do not speak the same language; and also anyone who can tell everything, now, or afterward, because they only have accidents and not what it is necessary for such disclosure.

In spite of the minor mysterious, they are the first to be preceded by pictures in modern times but not in all times, in addition to what is considered "pips," i.e. devices belonging to the percentages of different suits. These photos react to the divinatory meanings drawn from many sources. In summary, the present division of this key is thus dedicated to the Trump Major; in relation to the higher intent and in relation to the designs in the pack, it explains its cards. The third division will give the divinatory significance for the 78 Tarot cards and the designs of the Minor Arcana in particular. It will, in fine, give a few ways of use to those who need it and in the sense of the reason I explained in the preface. The foregoing should be taken for reference, in contrast to the general description in the first part of the old Tarot Trumps. There, the zero card of the Fool is assigned, as always, to the place which is equal to the number of twenty-one. The arrangement on the surface is ridiculous, which does not mean much, but it is also false on symbolism, nor is it better when the 22 second point of the sequence is replaced. Etteilla acknowledged the challenges of these two attributions, but only made it worse by assigning the Fool to the place that the Ace of Pentacles usually is the last one of the entire Tarot series. The new Papus in Le Tarot Divinatoire preceded this rearrangement, in which uncertainty is meaningless because the results of the plot rely on casual positions and not on a fundamental place in the general card series. I have seen another distribution of the zero symbol, which in some situations definitely is done, but it lacks on the highest levels, and it is idle to move further for our present requirements.

Section 2

THE TRUMP MAJOR AND THEIR INNER SYMBOLISM

ONE. THE MAGICIAN

What comes to fore is the image of a young man in the attire of a wizard with the mask of divine Apollo, a look of confidence and bright eyes. Above his head is the enigmatic symbol of the Holy Spirit, the sign of life in a horizontal position, as an infinite chain, shaping figure 8. A serpent-cincture is about his waist, and the serpent looks like his own tail. This is mostly recognized as a traditional representation of immortality, but here it most shows explicitly the eternity of accomplishment of the mind. In the right hand of the wizard is a wand held up to heaven while the left-hand points to the ground. This dual sign is known in the highest grades of the Instituted Mysteries; it displays the descent of grace, virtue, and light, derived from above and below. The suggestion is, therefore, the possession and communication of the Spirit's powers and gifts. The cards of the four Tarot suits stand on the table in front of the Magician, which represent elements of natural life that lie like counters to the adept, and he adapts them as he wishes. The roses and lily are below that, the flos cami and the lilium convallium, turned into garden flowers to display the aspiration society. This card reflects the religious intent of man, representing Christ in the deliverance of his union with the above. The cards unite the individual on every plane, and it is thought in a very high way in its fixation. Furthermore, as I called the sign of life and its relationship to number 8, it is remembered that Christian Gnosticism speaks of the rebirth in Christ as a change "to the Ogdoad." Above, the mystical number is called Jerusalem, a land flowing with milk and honey, the Holy Spirit, and the Land of the Lord. According to Martinism, 8 is Christ's number.

TWO. THE HIGH PRIESTESS

She has a lunar crescent at her feet, a horned diadem on her head, a globe on the center, and a large solar cross on her breast. The book in her hands is inscribed with the word Torah, which means the Grand Law, the Hidden Law, and the second part of the Word. It's partly covered by her mask to indicate that certain items are inferred and some spoken about. She stands between the black and white columns— J. and B.— The mystical Temple and the

Temple's veil are behind her: it's sticky with palm trees and grenades. The garments are fluid and gauzy, and the coat has a shiny light. She was called Occult Science on the threshold of the Shrine of Isis, but indeed she is the Secret Church, the House of God (Nature), and Man. The second marriage always reflects a Duke who is not of this world anymore; she is the divine Wife and Daughter, the daughter of the stars, and the Great Garden of Eden. She is the borrowed light Queen, in fine, but that is the light of all. She is the Moon fed by the Supernal Mother's milk.

In a way, she is the Supernal Mother herself— that is, the bright reflection. In this sense of meditation, Shekinah–the co-habiting beauty–is her truest and best name through the embolism. According to Kabalism, above and below, there is a Shekinah. In the higher universe, it is called the Binah, the supernal awareness that represents the fundamental emanations. Malkuth — the world to this end understood as a blessed Kingdom — is blessed with the Inner Glory in the lower world. Shekinah is the spiritual bride of the righteous man and gives Divine significance when he reads the Law. This card is the highest and most holy of the Greater Arcana, in some respects.

THREE. EMPRESS

A beautiful woman, sitting, with rich clothes and a royal appearance, like a divine and earthly friend. Its diadem is 12 stars, collected in a cluster. The Venus icon is on the shield above her. A field of corn ripens in front of it, and there is water falling beyond it. The wand she holds becomes overshadowed by the universe. The Earthly Paradise is the lower Garden of Eden, all that is symbolized by the recognizable man's house. She's not Empress Coeli, but the fruitful mother of thousands, the refuge peccatorum. Also, it is important to note that are certain aspects of the refuge peccatorum in which she was correctly described as the desire and its wings, like a woman wearing the sun, like Gloria Mundi and the veil of the Sanctum; but, I can add, the soul that reached its wings is not so, except as to count all the symbolism in a different and unusual way. It is above all divine vitality and the Word's outward meaning. This is apparent only because there is no direct message or information given to men as it was to women, but they don't interpret it themselves.

In another sequence of thoughts, the card of the Empress shows the path or gateway through which entry into this life is gained as in the Garden of Venus; and the way from it into that which is beyond, the key revealed to the high priestess is that it is transmitted by it to the chosen. Many of this card's old attributes are entirely wrong with symbolism, such as his identification with the Word, Divine Nature, triad, etc.

FOUR. THE EMPEROR

He has in his left hand a Crux ansata for his wand and a globe. He is a monarch-headed, ruling, seated on a throne, whose arms are faced by the heads of the rams. He's the executive and fulfillment, the power of the world, here wear the highest natural characteristics. He is sometimes portrayed as lying on a cubic stone that confuses some of the issues. He is the potent force the Empress refers to, and he wants to remove the Isis Veil in this way, but she remains virgin intact.

This symbol and that of the Empress, signifying the wife or partner, do not reflect the status of married life exactly, although this situation is inferred. On the surface, as I pointed out, they stand for worldly kingship, uplifted on the mighty's seats; but above that, there is the suggestion of another presence. They also mean — and especially the male figure— the higher kingship that occupies the intellectual throne. This is not the animal world but the lordship of thought. All minds, in their own way, are "full of strange knowledge," but the insight that emerges from a greater dimension is not aware of themselves. The Emperor has been described in its incarnated form as (a) will, but this is only one of his applications and (b) an expression of the virtualities in the Absolute Being — but this is fantasy.

FIVE. THE HIEROPHANT

He carries the triple crown and stands between two walls, but they're not those of the High Priestess ' Temple secured.And in his left hand which is the other hand, he holds a wand that ends in the triple cross, and with his right hand, he sets the well-known ecclesiastical sign called esotericism, which makes a distinction between the manifested and the hidden part of the teaching. In this connection, it is evident that the High Priestess does not make any sign. At his feet are the keys crossed and before him kneel two priestly ministers in albums. He was usually called the Pope, a particular expression of the more general office which he symbolizes. He is the dominant power of external religion, since high priestess is the commanding genius of esoteric, withdrawn power. The proper meanings of this card were admixtured by almost all hands. Great East actually says that the Hierophant is the powerful key, the orthodox, the exoteric doctrine, and the external side of life that leads to doctrine, but, as another commentator has suggested, he certainly is not the prince of occult belief.

It is rather the summa totius theologiæ when it has become the total rigidity of speech, but it also symbolizes all the good and holy things on the manifest line. As such, it is the source of grace that is different from the realm of government and the master of redemption for the human race as a whole. He is chief Order and the head of the recognized hierarchy which represents another and greater hierarchical order. But, this may happen when the Papal forgets the importance of his symbolic state and behaves as though he contains all that his sign implies, or his symbol attempts to represent, in his own steps. It's not philosophy, as it has been thought, except theology; it's not an inspiration; it's not religion, but it's a mode of its expression.

SIX. THE LOVERS

In the zenith, the sun shines, and below is a high winged figure with extended arms that pour out influences. There are two human figures in the foreground, male and female, revealed before each other as if Adam and Eve had first entered the earthly body's paradise. The Tree of Life, with twelve fruits, lies behind the man, and behind the woman is the Tree of the Knowledge of Good and Evil; the serpent is whirling around it. The symbol, figures and card suggest youth, virginity, innocence, and love before the gross material desire contaminates it. In all simplicity, this is the card of man's love, which is shown in the way, truth, and life. It replaces, by the use of first principles, the old marriage card which I have previously described and the subsequent madness that depicted man between vice and virtue. The card is, however, defined as a mystery of the Covenant and the Sabbath.

The suggestion regarding the woman is that it means that appeal to the sensitive life that carries within it the idea of the fall of man, but rather that it is the work of a Secret Law of Providence than a willing and conscious torment. It is through the imputed lapse that man ultimately emerges, and can only complete himself by her. The token is, therefore, another intimation of the great mystery of femininity in its own way. The old words fell into the old pictures of need, but even when reading the latter, some of them were of a specific nature, and others in language were incorrect.

SEVEN. THE CHARIOT

An erect and princely figure with a drawn sword and a conventional definition that compares, in general, to the one I gave in the first chapter. The Urim and Thummim should be on the shoulders of the victorious hero. He has conquered prison, conquered all planes — in mind, in science, in progress, in certain initiatory trials. He thus responded to the Sphinx, and I accepted the variation of Eliphas Lévi on that account; two sphinxes draw his chariot. He triumphs above all in the spirit.

It has, for this reason, (a) to be understood that the question of the Sphinx is about a Natural Mystery and not about the world of grace that the carriers can not answer; (b) that the planes of his conquest are manifest, outward, and not within themselves; (c) that his liberation can leave itself in the bondage of logical understanding; He is not an inherited kingdom, nor a priesthood.

EIGHT. STRENGTH AND FORTITUDE

A woman whose head is lined with the same sign of survival as we saw in the Hierophant's card shuts a lion's jaws. Only the advantage of its power has already overcome the lion, followed by a chain of flowers, is the distinction between this style and traditional presentations. The card was traded with that of Defense, which is typically numbered eight for purposes that please me. Since the variation has nothing to mean to the reader, there is no reason for an explanation. Fortitude, in one of its greatest dimensions, is associated with the Holy Unity of Union; virtue, of course, exists on every plane and therefore absorbs everybody in its meaning. It also deals with the purity of the untouched and the power of reflection.

However, these higher significances are deductible, and I do not suggest that they are transparent on the card surface. The chain of flowers instills you in a veiled way, which, among many other aspects, signifies the sweet yoga and light load of Divine Law, when carried into the heart of the heart. Although this has been suggested, the card has nothing to do with self-confidence in the ordinary sense— but it does concern the trust of those who have found their refuge in God (Nature). The lion means passions in one aspect, and the one called Strength is the highest nature in its release. He walked over the asp and basilisk and trampled down the lion and the dragon.

NINE. THE HERMIT

The difference from the conventional car versions is that the lamp is not partly covered in the robe of its holder, who incorporates the image of the Ancient of Ages with the world sun. It's a star shining in the lantern. I said this is a card of success, and to expand this creation, the character has eminence in its color. Therefore, the Hermit is not a wise man in the search for truth and justice, as Court de Gebelin explained; neither is he, as a later explanation suggests, a special example of experience. His beacon says that "when I'm here, you can be." It's also a card that's misunderstood when it's related to the idea of occult isolation, like protecting personal magnetism against admixture. This is one of Eliphas Lévi's trivial depictions. The French Martinism Order adopted it, and some of us heard much of the silent and unknown philosophy that is wrapped in its cloak from the insight of the profane. In real Martinism, the meaning of the unknown Philosopher was of a different order. It did not refer to the purpose to conceal the Instituted Mysteries, much less their replacements, but–as in the case of this card itself– the fact that the Divine Mysteries defend themselves against unprepared people.

TEN. WHEEL OF FORTUNE

I again pursued Eliphas Lévi's restoration, who furnished a number of variants. It is legitimate— as I have said — to use Egyptian symbolism, provided that it does not contain any origin theory. Yet I portrayed Typhon in the form of his snake. The symbolism is, obviously, not exclusively Egyptian as Ezekiel's four Living Creatures occupy the angles of the card, and as an illustration of Tarot Key, the wheel itself follows the indications of Lévi concerning Ezekiel's vision. The symbolic image stands in the French occultist and the design itself for the perpetual movement of a fluidic universe and the flow of human life. The Sphinx is the balance in it. The transliteration of Taro as Rota, compared with Divine Name letters, is inscribed on the wheel to demonstrate that Providence is implied in all. Morever, this is the divine and holy intention within, and without the like intention, the four living creatures are exemplified. The Sphinx is sometimes depicted couchant in the upper pedestal, which defrauds the symbolism by removing the basic concept of continuity of flight.

Behind the general notion of the symbol lies the denial of chance and the fatality implied in it. Additionally, the occult explanations of this card are of a singularly fatuous kind, even for occultism itself, from the days of Levi. It was said to mean principle, fertility, virile honor, governing authority, etc. The findings of common fortune-telling on their own planes are better than this.

ELEVEN. JUSTICE

As this card follows the traditional cards and carries above all their obvious meanings, there is nothing to say about it other than the few things that the reader refers to in the first part.

Nevertheless, it is obvious that the character is situated among the poles, such as the High Priestess, and it seems appropriate that the moral principle that extends to every person according to his or her actions, while of course in strict contrast, varies in nature from the divine justice involved in the notion of voting. The latter is part of a mysterious order of Providence that allows certain men to understand the idea of dedication to the highest things. It works like the breathing of the Soul where it wants, and we don't have any canon to condemn or justify it. It's analogous to the possession of the fairy gifts and the poet's great gifts and kind gifts: we either have them or not, and their presence is as mysterious as their absence. However, the law of justice does not involve either alternative. In conclusion, justice pillars open into one world, and the high priestess pillars into another.

TWELVE. THE HANGED MAN

The hanging gallows shapes a Tau symbol, whereas the man –from its leg position–forms a fylfot cross. A nimbus is around the head of the presumed martyr. (1) the tree of sacrifice is wood, with its leaves on it; (2) the face is a deep entry, not suffering;

(3) the figure suggests life suspended as a whole, but life and not death. It's a token of immense value, but it's all sealed. One of his editors says that the meaning of Eliphas Lévi is unquestionable — and the publisher himself did not. It was falsely called a "martyr card," a "prudence card," a "great work card," a "card of duty," but all published interpretations can be exhausted, and the only vanity can be found. On my own hand, I would say rather clearly that it reflects the bond between the Creator and the Earth in one of its dimensions.

Whoever will recognize that the message of his spiritual self is rooted in this symbolism gets intimations about a great potential rebirth, and he learns that there is a magnificent secret of the Resurrection after the holy mystery of death.

THIRTEEN. THE DEATH.

The mask or veil of life is perpetuated and enmeshed in change, transformation, and a passage from lower to higher realm, and this is more fittingly represented by one of the apocalyptic visions in the rectified Tarot than by the crude notion of the skeleton being reaped. The whole realm of metaphysical ascension lies behind it. The enigmatic horseman moves slowly, carrying a black flag that is decorated with the Mystic Rose, meaning life. The light of life shines between two pillars at the bottom of the horizon. The horseman does not hold any prominent hand, but the king and child and maiden fall before him, while his end awaits a prelate with clasped hands.

No need to point out that the implication of death that I made in connection with the previous card is, of course, to be mystically interpreted, but this is not the case in this instance. Man's natural movement to the next stage of his being is or may be one form of his development, but the exotic and almost unknown entry into the state of mystical death, while still in this life, is a change in the nature of consciousness and the transformation into a state, a place of absolute communion, in which ordinary death is neither the road nor the gate. Overall, the 13th card's current occult explanations are better than usual, regeneration, creation, destination, renewal, and the rest.

FOURTEEN. TEMPERANCE

A winged angel, the square and triangle of the septenary with the sign of the sun on his forehead and on his breast. In the masculine sense, I'm thinking about him, but the figure is not male or female. It is believed to be pouring from chalice to chalice, the essence of creation. It has one foot upon earth and one foot upon waters, thus illustrating the essences' nature. A straight path goes up to certain heights at the edge of the horizon, and there is a great light above, through which a crown is seen vaguely. Hereof is a part of the Secret of Eternal Life since his incarnation, and it is possible to man. Both traditional emblems are herewith renounced.

So are the traditional definitions, which refer to seasonal changes, life's constant shift, and even the combination of ideas. Furthermore, it is untrue to say that the figure symbolizes the sun's intellect even though it is the solar light comparison, realized in the third part of our human triplicity. It is called Temperance, fantastically, because it tempers, incorporates, and harmonizes the mental and material natures when the law of it obtains in our consciousness. Under that rule, we know something about where we came from and where we're going in our rational part.

FIFTEEN. THE DEVIL

The design is an accommodation between several motives mentioned in the first part, mean or harmony. The Horned Goat of Mendes sits on an altar, with wings identical to those of a bat. At the bottom, pit is the Mercury symbol. The right hand is uplifted and extended, the reverse of the blessing granted in the fifth card by the Hierophant. There is a great flaming torch in the left hand, inverted toward the earth. On the brow is a reversed pentagram. There is a ring before the altar, from which two chains, male and female, are held to the necks of two men. These are similar to those of the fifth coin, as if after the fall of Adam and Eve. Hereof is the chain of material life and its fatality.

The figures are tailed to signify animal nature, but the faces contain human intelligence, and he who is exalted above them will not be their master forever. He is also a bondman even now, sustained by the evil which is in him, and blind to the freedom of service. Eliphas Lévi, however, affirms that, also, the Baphometic figure is mystic science and sorcery, with more than his normal derision for the arts, which he claimed to admire and view as a master therein. Another commentator says it means predestination in the Divine world, but there is no correspondence in that world with the brute things below. What it means is the Dweller without the Mystical Garden on the Threshold when those who have consumed the forbidden fruit are forced out of it.

SIXTEEN. THE TOWER

Occult explanations are meager and most disconcerting, attached to this card. It is idle to suggest that it depicts ruin in all its aspects because on the surface, it carries the truth. It is further said that it contains the first allusion to a building of materials, but I do not conceive that the Tower is more or less material than the pillars we have met in three preceding cases. I don't see anything to warrant Papus in assuming it's literally Adam's fall, but there's more to his alternative — that it means the spiritual world is materialized.

The Christian bibliographer imagines it is the weakness of the spirit, trying to explore the mystery of God (Nature). I rather agree with the Greater Orient that it is the ruin of the House of Life, when evil has prevailed therein, and above all, that it is the rendering of a House of Doctrine. However, I understand the reference is to a House of Falsehood. It also shows in the most detailed way the old reality that "with the exception of the Lord building the house, they labor in vain to build this." There is a context in which the tragedy is a continuation from the previous card, but not on the side of the meaning I tried to suggest. It is a matter of analogy more correctly; one is concerned with falling into the material and animal environment, while the other is intellectual devastation. The Tower was spoken of as the chastisement of ego and the exhausted intellect to penetrate the Mysteries of God (Nature), but in no case do these theories account for the two individuals who are the living sufferers. The one is the word that has been avoided, and the other its false interpretation. It may also mean the end of a dispensation in a still deeper sense, but there is no possibility here to answer this involved issue.

SEVENTEEN. THE STAR

A great, eight-ray, radiant star, surrounded by seven lesser stars— also eight rays. In the background, the female figure is absolutely naked. Her left knee is on the ground, with her right foot on the water. She pours out two great ewers of Water of Life, irrigating the sea and the land. A shrub or tree rises up behind her, to the right, where a bird alights. The figure is expressive of eternal beauty and youth. The star is l'étoile flamboyante, used in Masonic symbolism but confused therein. The substance of the heavens and the elements is that which the figure communicates to the living scene. Truly it has been said that this card's mottoes are "Waters of Life Free" and "Gifts of the Spirit." The summary of several tawdry explanations says it's a card of hope. It has been certified as immortality on other planes and as an interior light. For most prepared minds, the figure will appear as the unveiled type of Truth, glorious in undying beauty, pouring some part and measure of her priceless possession on the waters of the soul. But in reality, she is the Great Mother in the Kabalistic Sephira Binah, which is supernal Understanding, who communicates to the

Sephiroth who are below to the extent they can receive her highest influx of power.

EIGHTEEN. THE MOON

The distinction between this card and some of the conventional types is that the moon grows to the right of the observer, on what is called the side of mercy. It has seventeen secondary rays, and seventeen. The card depicts fantasy life apart from spiritual life. The path between the towers is the problem towards what is unknown. The wolf and the dog are the deep fears of natural mind when it is only reflected light to guide it in the presence of that place of exit.

The last reference is the key to a different kind of symbolism. The mental light is a reflection, and the hidden mystery that it can not disclose is beyond it. It illuminates our animal nature, forms of which are represented below — the horse, the wolf, and that which rises from the sea, the nameless and hideous instinct which is lower than the wild animal. It aims to achieve realization, symbolized by creeping into the land from the depths of darkness, but as a rule, it falls down from where it came from. The face of the mind directs a steady eye on the turmoil below; the dew of thought falls; the message is harmony, stillness; and it may be that the nature of the animal will be still, while the void below will cease to offer up a form.

NINETEEN. THE SUN

The naked child mounted on a white horse, and showing a red standard has already been mentioned as the better symbolism linked to this card. It is the fate of the Supernatural East and the sacred and holy light that goes before the endless procession of mankind, coming out of the delicate life's walled garden and going on the journey home. Consequently, the card signifies the transit from the manifest light of this world, represented by the glorious sun of earth, to the light of the world to come, which precedes aspiration and is typified by a child's heart.

But the last allusion is yet again the key to a different symbolism form or aspect. The sun is that of spirit-consciousness— the direct as the antithesis of the reflected light. In it, humanity's characteristic type has become a little child— a child in the sense of simplicity and innocence in the sense of wisdom. He bears the seal of Nature and Art in that simplicity; in that innocence, he means the restored world. When the self-knowing spirit has dawned above the human mind in the consciousness, the mind in its regeneration brings forth animal nature in a state of complete conformity.

TWENTY. THE LAST JUDGEMENT

This card is practically invariable in all Tarot sets, or at least its character is not altered by the variations. Clouds surround the great angel here. However, he blasts his bannered trumpet, and the cross is depicted on the banner as usual. The dead are emerging from their graves— a woman on the right, a man on the left, and their infant between them, whose back is turned. But there are more than three that are restored in this card, and making this variation as an illustration of the insufficiency of current explanations has been thought worthwhile. It should be noted that all of the figures are expressed by their attitudes as one in wonder, adoration, and ecstasy. It is the card that documents the accomplishment of the great work of transformation in response to the summons of the

Supernal — which is heard and answered from within.

Here is the intimation of a sense that in the present position can not be carried on. What's that within us that sounds a trumpet and everything that's lower in our existence rises in response — nearly in a moment, almost in an eye's twinkling? Let the card continue to portray the Last Judgment and the resurrection in the natural body for those who can not see any further, but let those who have inward eyes look and discover with it. They will understand that it was truly called a card of eternal life in the past, and for this reason, it can be compared with what passes under the name Temperance.

TWENTY-ONE. THE FOOL

With a light step, as if the earth and its trammels had little power to restrain him, a young man in beautiful clothes stands at the edge of a precipice among the world's great heights; he is watching the blue space before him— the expanse of heaven rather than the possibility below. His act of eager walking is still suggested, though, at the given moment, he is stationary; his dog is still bounded. The edge that opens into the depth has no terror; it's as if angels were waiting to safeguard him if it happened that he sprang from the height. His face is full of wisdom and a vision of hope. For he has a flower rose in one hand, and an expensive wand in the other, from which an oddly embroidered wallet rests upon his right shoulder. He's a prince of the other world on his journeys through this one— all in the glory of the morning, in the fierce air. The sun, shining behind him, knows where he came from, where he's going to go, and how after many days, he's going to return by another path. He's the one that's searching for knowledge. Many Instituted Mysteries cards are summarized in this card, reversing all the confusions that preceded it under high warrants.

Grand Orient has a curious suggestion of Mystic Fool's office as part of his process in higher divination in his Manual Of Cartomancy, but it may require more than ordinary gifts to put it into operation. We will see how the card ranks according to the traditional arts of fortune-telling, and it will be an indication to those who can discern that the Trump Major had no place in the arts of supernatural gambling when cards are used as counters and pretexts, otherwise so obvious. But we know very little about the conditions under which this art originated. The conventional explanations say that the Fool stands for the flesh, the sensitive life, and its subsidiary name was at one time the alchemist by a peculiar satire, as it depicts folly at the most senseless stage.

TWENTY TWO. THE WORLD

As the Major Trumps ' final message remains unchanged—and indeed unchangeable—with regard to its nature, it has already been partly identified with regard to its deeper sense. It also reflects the creation and end of the Universe, the mystery within it, the rapture of the world when it in God (Nature) knows itself. It is, however, the state of the soul in Divine Vision consciousness, reflected from the spirit of self-knowledge. But those meanings are without prejudice.

On the macrocosmic side, it has more than one message and is, for example, the state of the restored world when the law of manifestation has been carried to the highest degree of natural perfection. But perhaps it is more specifically a story of the past, referring to that day when everything was declared good when the morning stars were singing together, and all the Sons of God (Nature) were shouting for joy. One of the worst theories about it is that the figure symbolizes the Magus when it hits the highest degree of initiation; another account says it reflects the absolute, which is ludicrous. The number has been said to stand for reality, which is assigned to the seventeenth card more accurately, however. It was, lastly, dubbed the Magi's Crown.

Section 3

THE CONCLUSION IN RELATION TO THE GREATER KEYS

In the previous chapter there was no attempt to present the meaning in what is considered the three worlds— that of God, the Macrocosm, and the Microcosm. For developments of this kind a large volume would be needed. I took the cards of their more direct significance to man on the high plane, who is in the quest for eternal things— in material life—. The one who is the compiler of the Book Of Cartomancy has categorized them under three headings: the World of Human Prudence, which on its more serious side is no different from divination; the World of Conformity, being the life of religious devotion; and the World of Attainment, which is that of "the progress of the soul towards the end of its research." I do not have such process to offer, as I believe that individual reflection on each of the Trump Major could gain more. Also, I have not adopted the prevailing allocation of Hebrew alphabet cards— firstly because it would not serve any purpose in an elementary handbook; secondly, because almost every attribution, however, is wrong. Finally, I do not attempt to rectify the placement of the cards in their connection to each other; therefore the Zero occurs after No. 20, but I have taken care not to list the Planet or Earth other than as 21. The Zero is an unnumbered card, wherever it should be put.

To conclude with regard to this part, I will give these additional indications regarding the Fool, which is the most frequently spoken of all cards. He signifies the outward journey, the state of the first emanation, the spirit's graces and passivity. His pocket is decorated with flickering signals that indicate that the mind retains other secret memories.

PART III

THE OUTER METHOD OF THE ORACLES

Section 1

DIFFERENCE BETWEEN THE GREATER AND LESSER ARCANA

In spite of their healthy appearance, tarot cards—King, Queen, Knight and Squire or Page — provide the connection between the Greater and the Lesser Arcana. Yet, their absolute difference from the Trump Major is shown by their traditional form. Let the reader compare them with Cards like the Fool, the High Priestess, the Hierophant, or in the previous sequence, almost without exception, and he will discern my meaning. There is no special idea connected to the ordinary court cards on the surface; they are a bridge of conventions forming a transition to the simple pretexts of the counters and denarii of the numbers that follow. We seem to have completely passed on from the area of higher significances demonstrated by living images.

Nevertheless, there was a moment when the numbered cards were also images, but such instruments were different artists ' intermittent creations and were either traditional or allegorical standard compositions, distinct from what symbolism knows, or were illustrations— shall we say?—of traditions, etiquette, and times. They were adornments, in a phrase, and as such, they did nothing to raise the importance of the Lesser Arcana to the Trump Major plane; however, these variations are extremely rare. Nevertheless, in the minor cards, there are vague rumors about a higher meaning, but nothing has transpired so far, even within the sphere of prudence that belongs to the most occult circles; these, it is true, have some variants with respect to divinatory values, but I have not heard that they offer better results in practice.

Efforts such as those of Papus in The Tarot Of The Bohemians are strenuous and deserving of their own kind. They are identified as the elements of the Divine Immanence in the Trump Major and tries to pursue them through the long series of the lesser cards, as if these constituted filtrations of the State of Grace through the Land of Fortune. Yet, he creates only an arbitrary scheme of the lesser cards. Today, I'm basically in the same position. Still, I'm not going to make any effort here to save the condition by relying on numbers ' magical properties as he and others have attempted.

We should acknowledge that the Trump Major belongs to the divine transactions of philosophy, but all that follows fortune-telling since it has never yet been translated into another language; the course thus adopted will render to divination, and even to gambling, the things that belong to this particular world of skill, and will distinguish those things for their proper business. In this free introduction to the subject in hand, it is only necessary to add that the difference between the fifty-six Lesser Arcana and the ordinary play-cards is not only slight, because the replacement of Cups for Hearts and so on is an accidental variation, but also because the presence of a Knight in each of the four suits was characteristic at one time of many ordinaries. In the rectified Tarot describing the present handbook, all numbered cards of the Lesser Arcana — with the exception of the Aces only — are presented with figures or pictures to demonstrate, but without wasting, the divinatory significance added to them.

Some who in more than the ordinary sense are blessed with analytical and discerning faculties—

and I am not speaking of clairvoyance — may note that in many of the Lesser Arcana, there are ambiguous intimations transmitted by the designs that seem to surpass the divinatory values specified. It is important to prevent confusion by certainly stating that the deviations are not to be regarded as signs of higher and extra-divinatory meaning, except in rare instances — and then only through mistake. I said these Lesser Arcana were not translated into a language that transcends the language of fortune-telling.

Yes, I should not be inclined to treat them as belonging to a world other than this in their present forms; but the scope of divinatory possibilities is inexhaustible, by the theory of history, and the integrated schemes of cartomancy have shown only the bare heads of importance attached to the emblems in use. In the present case, when the pictures go beyond the conventional meanings, they should be taken as hints of possible developments along the same lines; and this is one of the reasons why the pictorial devices attached here to the four denaries will be of great help to the intuition.

The mere numerical powers and naked words of the meanings are by themselves insufficient, but the pictures are like doors opening into unexpected chambers, or like a turn on the open road with a wide prospect beyond.

Section 2

THE LESSER ARCANA

Otherwise the Four Suits of Tarot Cards will now be described by the pictures of each belonging according to their respective classes, and a harmony of their meanings from all sources will be given.

Such are the Lesser Arcana's intimations regarding divinatory art, the veridical nature of which appears to depend on an alternative that can be useful for brief expression. The art documents are ex hypothesis the archives of previous experience-based findings; as such, they are a reference to recollection, and those who can learn the elements will, on their basis, provide explanations — even ex hypothesis—. It is an automatic and official working process. On the other side, those who have gifts of perception, of second sight, of clairvoyance— call it as we choose and can — will augment the knowledge of the past with the observations of their own senses, and will talk about what they saw in the pretexts of the oracles. It remains to offer the divinatory meaning which the same art assigns to the Trump Major, even briefly.

THE SUITS OF WANDS.

WANDS. KING.

The physical and emotional nature attributed to this card is dark, ardent, lithe, animated, impassioned and noble. The King raises a budding staff, and, like his three correspondences in the remaining uniforms, sports what is considered a care cap under his crown. He interacts with the lion's emblem which is emblazoned on his throne's neck.

Divinatory meanings: Dark man, friendly, countryman, married, honest and conscientious in general. The card also implies integrity, and may mean that reports about an unlikely ancestry should come in very shortly.

Inverted: Nice, yet harsh; austere, but receptive.

WANDS. QUEEN.

The Wands are always in the leaf throughout this suit, as it is a trait of life and animation. The Queen's personality, emotionally and otherwise, corresponds to that of the King, but is more magnetic.

A dark lady, country-woman, sweet, chaste, caring, noble. If the card next to her shows an individual, she will be well inclined towards him; if a woman is interested in the Querent. Love for wealth, or some success in business, too.

Reversed: Nice, cost-effective, serviceable, mandatory. It also implies resistance, resentment, even hypocrisy and infidelity— but in some places and in the area of other cards tending in such directions.

WANDS. KNIGHT.

He's shown as though mounted with a small wand on a ride, and though mailed is not on a warlike errand. He's passing around mounds or pyramids. The horse's motion is a key to his rider's character, and suggests the precipitate mood, or things related to it.

Divinatory Meanings: Departure, travel, absence, emigration. A handsome, dark young man. Changing of spot.

Reversed: Rupture, Split, Conflict.

WANDS. PAGE.

A young man stands in an act of proclamation in a scene like the former. He is unknown but loyal, and his news is odd.

Divinatory means: a dark, faithful young man, a lover, a messenger, a postman. He will bear favorable testimony about him besides a man. A risky opponent, if the Cups link is followed. Has his suit's main qualities. He can mean intelligence of the family.

Reversed: Anecdotes, commercials, bad news. Indecision and the accompanying instability.

WANDS. TEN.

A man constrained by the weight of the 10 bars he bears.

Divinatory Interpretations: a card with many interpretations and readings that can not be harmonized. I set aside the connection between honor and good faith. The key definition is literally oppression, but it is also wealth, income and any form of achievement, therefore oppression. It's also a card of false, cover-up, perfidy. The position the figure approaches may be influenced by the rods he

holds. Success is stultified when the Nine of the Swords follows and there will be a certain loss if it is a matter of a lawsuit.
Reversed: inconsistencies, problems, storylines and analogies.

WANDS. NINE.

The character leans on his staff and looks waiting like an enemy is waiting. There are eight other staves behind—upright, orderly, like a palisade.
Divinatory Meanings: The card reflects opposition power. When attacked, the person met an assault boldly, and his construction showed he could prove a tremendous antagonist. With this main importance all possible additional elements are available—delay, suspension, delay.
Reversed: obstructions, hardship, catastrophe.

WANDS. EIGHT.

The card represents movement through the immovable— a flight of walls through an open country, but draws at the end of its course. What they mean is near; it may even be at the threshold.

Divinatory meanings: business activity, the way for such activities, speed as the express messenger, great eagerness, great hope, speed to an end that promises guaranteed congratulatoryness; in general, what is in motion; even the arrows of love. Reversed: envy missiles, domestic disputes, aware stinging, quarrels; and domestic disputes among married people.

WANDS. SEVEN.

A young man brandishing a staff on a messy eminence; six other staves are pushed from below towards him.

Divinatory Meanings: It's a valence card, for six attack one on the surface, but one with the vantage point. It means debate, wordy dispute on the intellectual plane. In business — negotiations, trade war, trade, competition. It is also a victory card because the combatant is at the top and his opponents may not be able to reach him.

Reversed: uncertainty, confusion, anxiety. It also represents a warning against indecision.

WANDS. SIX.

A laurel horseman has a staff crowned with a laurel crown. There are staff footmen on his side.

Divinatory Meanings: The card has been designed to cover many meanings: on the surface it triumphs, but also great news that the king's courier will bring in state; hopes crowned with its own wish, the crown of hope, and so on.

Reversed: anxiety, terror, like a triumphant enemy at the gate; treachery, disloyalty, opening the gate to the enemy.

WANDS. FIVE.

A picture of young people who brandish their workers as though they were in competition or hardship. It is an imitation of war and the Divinatory Meansings refer to this: imitation, like, for example, the false battle, but also the strenuous struggle and combat of the quest for wealth and fortune. It connects with the battle of life in this sense. Therefore, certain attributes say it is a gold card, gain, opulence.

Reversed: Litigation, choas, trickery, conflict.

WANDS. FOUR.

There is a wide guirland suspended from the four broad staves in the front; two female figures lift their nosegays; a bridge is on their side over a moat leading to an old manor house.

Divinatory Meanings: they are almost on the surface, for once— country life, shelter, domestic harvest-home animals, rest, harmony, prosperity, peace and their perfect work.

Reversed: The sense remains unchanged: wealth, development, happiness, beauty, enhancement.

WANDS. THREE.

A cool, beautiful person, turned his back, staring from the edge of a cliff at sea ships. In the ground three bars are planted, and he leans slightly on one.

Divinatory Meanings: he symbolizes established power, organization, commitment, enterprise, trade, business, discovery; those are his ships carrying his goods sailing across the seas. The card also means collaboration in company, as if the prosperous merchant prince looked towards you from his side to help you.

Reversed: end of trouble, suspension or cessation of adversity, labor and deception.

WANDS. TWO.

A tall man looks over the sea and the shore from the beating wall, he holds the globe on his right hand, while on the beat there is a staff in his left hand. Rose and Cross and Lily on the left side should be noticed. Divinatory meanings: no possible marriage is possible between alternative readings; on the one hand, wealth, fortune, glory; on the other hand, physical distress, disease, sorrow, sadness, mortifications. The concept implies one thing; here is a lord who overlooks his law and looks at a globe; he looks like Alexander's malady, mortification, sorrow in the grandeur of the riches of this nation. Reversed: Surprise, wonder, joy, emotion, anxiety, fear.

WANDS. ACE.

A cloud hand grasps a stout wall or club. ACE. Divinatory meanings: creation, invention, enterprise, the forces that result in them, principle, beginning, source; birth, family, source and, in some sense, virility behind them; the point of departure of companies; money, fortune, heritage, according to another account.

Reversed: Fall, decay, ruin, perdition, perishing; also some clouded joy.

THE CUPS SUIT.

CUPS. KING.

A small wand is holding him in his left hand and a large cup on his right; his throne is on the sea; there is a ship on one side riding and the dolphin on the other. The implication is that the sign of the cup refers naturally to water, which is reflected in all court cards.

Divinatory meanings: equal man, businessman, law, or divinity; responsible for convincing Querent; equity, art, and science, including professors of science, law, and art; artistic intelligence.

Dishonest, two-handed; rogue, exaction, injustice, vice, outrage, looting, significant loss.

CUPS. QUEEN.

Lovely, fair, dreamy—as someone who sees dreams in a cup. However, this is just one part of her: she sees nor acts, and her action nourishes her dream.

Divinatory Meanings: Good, fair woman; honest, devoted woman, who will do service to the Querent; loving intelligence, and hence the gift of vision; success, happiness, pleasure; also wisdom, virtue; a perfect spouse and a good mother.

Reversed: The accounts vary; good woman; otherwise, distinguished woman but one not to be trusted; perverse woman; vice, dishonor, depravity.

CUPS. KNIGHT.

Graceful, but not warlike; riding quietly, wearing a winged helmet, referring to those higher graces of the imagination which sometimes characterize this card. He too is a dreamer, but the images of the side of sense haunt him in his vision.

Divinatory Meanings: Arrival, approach — sometimes that of a messenger; advances, proposition, demeanor, invitation, incitement.

Reversed: Trickery, artifice, subtlety, swindling, duplicity, fraud.

CUPS. PAGE.

A fair, pleasing, somewhat effeminate page, of studious and intent aspect, contemplates a fish rising from a cup to look at him. It is the pictures of the mind taking form.

Divinatory Meanings: Fair young man, one impelled to render service and with whom the Querent will be connected; a studious youth; news, message; application, reflection, meditation; also these things directed to business.

Reversed: Taste, inclination, attachment, seduction, deception, artifice.

CUPS. TEN.

Appearance of Cups in a rainbow; it is contemplated in wonder and ecstasy by a man and woman below, evidently husband and wife. His right arm is about her; his left is raised upward; she raises her right arm. The two children dancing near them have not observed the prodigy but are happy after their own manner. There is a home-scene beyond.

Divinatory Meanings: Contentment, repose of the entire heart; the perfection of that state; also perfection of human love and friendship; if with several picture-cards, a person who is taking charge of the Querent's interests; also the town, village or country inhabited by the Querent.

Reversed: Repose of the false heart, indignation, violence.

CUPS. NINE.

A goodly personage has feasted to his heart's content, and abundant refreshment of wine is on the arched counter behind him, seeming to indicate that the future is also assured. The picture offers the material side only, but there are other aspects.

Divinatory Meanings: Concord, contentment, physical bien-être; also victory, success, advantage; satisfaction for the Querent or person for whom the consultation is made.

Reversed: Truth, loyalty, liberty; but the readings vary and include mistakes, imperfections, etc. CUPS.

CUPS. EIGHT.

A man of dejected lands is leaving, rejecting the cups of his felicity, enterprise, undertaking or previous concern in this card.

Divinatory Meanings: This card carefully speaks for itself on the surface, however, other readings are entirely antithetical— giving joy, mildness, timidity, honor, modesty. In practice, it is usually found that the cards.

CUPS. SEVEN

This brings a strange chalices of vision and imagery, however, the imagery are in their numbers, especially those of the fantastic spirit.

Divinatory Meanings: Favors of and from Fairy, imagery of introspection, sentiment, intuition, things seen in the glass of contemplation; some achievement in these degrees, but nothing permanent or substantial is suggested.

Reversed: wish, will, determination, project.

CUPS. SIX.

Children, their cups full of flowers in an old garden.

Divinatory meanings: card of the past and of the memories, looking back, such as childhood; happiness, pleasure, but rather past; things that have disappeared. This is reversed by another reading, which gives new relationships, new knowledge, a new environment and then the children sport in a familiar place.

Reversed: the future, regeneration, what will happen right now.

CUPS. FIVE.

A dark, shrouded man who looks at three cups at each side; two others stand upright behind him; the bridge is in the distance, leading to a small hold or holding.

Divinatory Meansings: It's a card of loss, but there's still something to stay with, three have been taken, but two are left, it's a card of heritage, heritage, and transmission that's not in line with expectations.

Reversed: reporting, alliances, affiliation, heritage, back, false ventures.

CUPS. FOUR.

A young man sits under a tree and looks at three cups set in front of him on a grass; another cup is given to his arm out of a cloud. FOUR. Despite his language, he is unhappy with his climate.

Divinatory meaning: fatigue, disgust, aversion, imaginary vexations, as if the wine of this world had only caused satiety. A wastrel is now being offered to another wine as if a fairy gift, but there is no consolation. This is also a mixed fun coin.

Reversed: news, forecasts, new orders, new relationships.

CUPS. THREE.

Maidens raised in a garden with cups, as if they were pledging each other.

Divinatory means: the conclusion of everything in abundance, perfection, and merriment; joy, victory, fulfilment, comfort, healing.

Reversed: Expedition, shipment, performance, end. It also means the excess side in physical

CUPS. TWO.

A young man and a maid pledge each other and the Caduceus of Hermes stands above their cups, between which the big wings are lion's head. It is a variation of a sign found in some old card examples. It has some curious emblematic definitions, but they do not affect us here.

Divinatory meanings: affection, passion, fellowship, affinity, peace, compassion, the relationship of gender and, in addition to all divine offices, the desire that is not natural but through which nature is sanctified. Divinatory meanings:

CUPS. ACE.

The waters are under, there are water lilies thereon: the hand comes from the cloud and holds the cup in his palm, from which four streams flow; the dove, bearing a cross-marked host in his bank, descends and places the wafer in the cup; the dew of water droppes on all sides. ACE. It is a reminder of what lies behind the Lesser Arcana.

Divine Meaning: Real Heart Home, happiness, contentment, abode, fruit, abundance, fertility; Holy Tables, congratulations hereof.

Reversed: False heart building, mutation, anarchy, revolt.

THE SUIT OF SWORDS.

SWORDS. KING.

He sits in judgment and holds his suit's unsheathed sign. He clearly recalls the traditional Symbol of Justice in the Trump Major and may stand for this ideal, but by virtue of his office he is rather the force of life and mortality.

Divinatory Meanings: Which emerges from the concept of judgment and all its associations—control, order, influence, activist intellect, law, crown offices, etc.

Cruel, perversity, barbarism, perplexity, evil intent.

SWORDS. QUEEN

Her right hand raises the gun vertically, and her hilt rests on the arm of her royal chair; her left hand extends, her arm lifts up, her face is serious, but her face is chastened. It does not signify compassion, and with its shield, it is hardly a power emblem.

Widowhood, female sorrow and humiliation, poverty, sterility, grief, suffering, separation. Divinatory means:

Reversed: malice, bigotry, explosions, prudery, bale, deception.

SWORDS. KNIGHT.

He's traveling in full direction, as if his rivals were scattered. He is really a proto-typical hero of romantic chivalry in architecture. He may be nearly Galahad, whose sword is quick and sure because he's clean of heart.

Ability, courage, skill, protection, adress, enmity, wrath, battle, devastation, resistance and ruin. The card thus means death, but it only has this significance in its relation to other cards of fatality.

Reversed: insensitivity, incapacity, extravagance.

SWORDS. PAGE.

A light, active figure carries a sword in both hands upright while walking quickly. He crosses rugged land and the clouds are randomly positioned around him. He's vigilant and alert, looking this way, as if a potential threat could ever appear.

Divinatory Meanings: Authority, supervision, secret service, alertness, spying, examination and their qualities.

Reverse: More unexpected, inexperienced side of these qualities; illness is also intimated.

SWORDS. TEN.

A prostrate figure, pierced with all of the card's swords.

Divinatory meanings: design intimates whatever; also pain, distress, tears, sorrow, desolation. It's not just a violent death card.

Reversed: benefit, income, prosperity, popularity, but none of these is permanent, wealth and strength as well.

SWORDS. NINE.

One sat in lamentation on her sofa with swords over it. She is like one who knows no sorrow like her. It's a total desolation coin.

Death, failure, miscarriage, delay, deception, deception, desperation.

Reversed: jail, suspicion, doubt, reasonable fear, shame.

SWORDS. EIGHT.

A woman, bound and hoodwinked, with her card's swords. Furthermore, it is more a temporary token than a permanent slavery.

Divinatory Meanings: Bad news, violent sorrow, crisis, censorship, tram force, dispute and slander; illness as well.

Reversed: Disquiet, trouble, opposition, accident, tragedy; the unforeseen; death.

SWORDS. SEVEN.

A man holding five swords quickly; the rest of the card remains trapped in the dirt. A camp is near by.

Divinatory means: concept, attempt, wish, hope, trust; quarrels; a strategy that could fail and annoyance. The design is uncertain, as the significance varies widely from one another.

Good advice, advice, preparation, gossip, babbling.

SWORDS. SIX.

A ferryman carrying passengers to another shore at his punt. The path is smooth and, since the freight is light, the job can not be taken for granted.
Divinatory Significance: Water path, road, route, ambassador, administrator, expedient.
Reversed: argument, confidence, advertising; one account says it is a love proposal.

SWORDS. FIVE.

Two authoritarian and dejected figures are taken care of by a disdainful man. Their blades lie on the floor. He is holding on his left shoulder two swords, and the third sword is pointed at the ground with his right hand. He's the master who owns the ground.
Divinatory Significances: degradation, destruction, revocation, infamy, dishonor and loss with their variants and analogs.
Reversed: the same; burial and gifts.

SWORDS. FOUR.

The knight's effigy in prayer pose, at his grave in full length.

Divinatory Meanings: watchfulness, isolation, loneliness, resting, exile, grave and sarcophagus. The last ones suggested the design.

Reversed: wise management, circumstance, economics, greed, caution, will.

SWORDS. THREE.

Three swords piercing the heart, and behind them cloud and rain.

Divinatory Significances: elimination, absence, pause, separation, rupture, dispersion and all of which are normal, are too simple and clear to be enumerated.

Reversed: Psychological detachment, mistake, loss, diversion, distraction, uncertainty.

SWORDS. TWO.

Two swords are on her back by a hoodwinked female figure.

The divinative meanings: the discipline and the equipment that it provides, bravery, peace and unity in a state of war. The suggestion of harmony and other favorable interpretations must be taken into account in a qualified manner, since Swords are generally not symbolic of benevolent forces in human matters.

Reversed: falsity, duplicity, disloyalty, falsehood.

SWORDS. ACE.

A hand emerges from a cloud, grasping a sword, whose point is surrounded by a crown.

Triumph, excessive degree in everything, victory, triumph of power. It is a card of great strength, both in love and in hate. The crown may have a much greater importance than is usually found in the sphere of fortune-telling.

Reversed: the same, but the results are disastrous; another account says: conception, birth, rise, multiplicity.

THE SUIT OF PENTACLES.

PENTACLES. KINGS.

This image has a dark face, which indicates bravery, and the bull's head should be remembered on the throne as a recurring emblem. The symbol of this suit is depicted as the pentigram grafted, which typifies the communication and governance between the four elements of human nature. This suit represented money in old Tarot packs. The consensus of divinatory significance is on the side of change, because the cards do not address money issues in particular.

Divinatory meanings: courage, intelligence, business, mathematical gifts and success.

Vice, weakness, perversity, danger.

PENTACLES. QUEEN.

This face reflects that of a mysterious woman, whose virtues can be summed up in the notion of superiority of mind. She also has a significant cast of intellect.

Divinatory meanings: opulence, kindness, splendor, protection, independence.

Reversed: Bad, distrust, suspicion, fear, mistrust.

PENTACLES. KNIGHT.

He's riding a sluggish, enduring, heavy horse, which correlates to his own dimension. He reveals his mark, but doesn't look inside.

Divinatory meanings: value, ability to serve, purpose, obligation, correctness— all on the usual or external level.

Reversed: boredom, idleness, this kind of rest, stagnation; even complacency, discouragement, carelessness.

PENTACLES. PAGE.

A young person who looks closely at the pentacle over his face. He's moving slowly, oblivious to what's around him.

Divinatory Meanings: application, study, scholarship and reflection; another reading tells you news, messages and the person who brings them; it also rules and governs.

Reversed: Displeasure, liberality, privilege, unfavorable news.

PENTACLES. TEN.

A man and a woman under an archway that leads to a house and domain. They are accompanied by a kid who curiously looks at two dogs, a former person sitting in the foreground. One of them is the hand of the boy.

Divinatory meanings: income, wealth; family affairs, records, extraction; family residence.

Reversed: Opportunity, death, loss, theft, danger games; sometimes gift, dowry, pension.

PENTACLES. NINE.

A woman with a bird on her arm is standing in the garden of a manor house in the midst of the great abundance of grape vines. It's a wide field that suggests lots of things. Perhaps it is her own property and shows material well-being.

Divinatory Meanings: Caution, safety, success, achievement, certainty, discernment.

Reversed: Roguery, frustration, mission zero, bad faith.

PENTACLES. EIGHT.

A stone artist in his work, displayed as trophies.
Significance: work, work, contract, design, craft and business skills, perhaps in the preparatory stage.
Reversed: Ambitious vacuum, arrogance, greed, exaction, usury. In the sense of the inventive mind turned to art and mystery, it can also mean the possession of skills.

PENTACLES. SEVEN.

A young person, leaning on the staff, looks at seven pentacles attached to a green clump to his right. You might say these were his jewels and his heart was there.
Divinatory means: they are extremely contradictory; they are, in the main, a card of money, company, barter, but a reading gives an argument, a dispute, an innocence, naivety and purgation.
Reversed: source of anxiety about the money that could be given.

PENTACLES. SIX.

A person weights the money in a pair of scales as a merchant, and distributes it to the poor and afflicted. It is a testimony to his own achievement and goodness of heart in life.

Divinatory means: present, gifts, satisfaction; another account states attention, vigilance; the time is now accepted, prosperity is present, etc.

Reversed: Wish, greed, envy, jealousy, illusion.

PENTACLES. FIVE.

Two mendicants pass an illuminated casement in a snowstorm.

Divinatory Meansings: The card predicts material problems specifically, whether in the manner depicted, i.e., suffering or otherwise. It's a love card to some cartomancists, and lovers–the wife, boyfriend, mate, mistress; concordance, affinities, too. Unable to harmonize these alternatives.

Reversed: Disorder, chaos, destruction, strife, frustration.

PENTACLES. FOUR.

Another man clasps with hands and arms with one crowned figure with a pentacle above his crown; two pentacles are under his feet. He's holding what he's got.

Divinatory Meanings: protection of land, loyalty to what one has, gift, legacy, heritage.

Suspense, delay, opposition.

PENTACLES. THREE.

A sculptor at a monastery's job. Compare the design of the Eight Pentacles. The pupil or novice got his reward and is now seriously involved.

Divinatory meanings: Metry, trade and skilled labor; but commonly seen as nobility's coin, aristocracy, prestige, glory.

Reversed: media, functioning and otherwise, puerility, sluggishness, weakness.

PENTACLES. TWO.

A young man has the pentacle in either hand in the act of dancing, and they are joined by that infinite cord which resembles the number 8.

Divinatory meanings: It is, on the one hand, a card of gaiety, recreation and its relationships that is the subject of design; it is also read as news and messages in writing, as hindrance, agitation, trouble, confusion.

Reversed: enforced enjoyment, simulated enjoyment, literal meaning, handwriting, composition, exchange letters.

PENTACLES. ACE.

A hand — raised from a globe, as normal — carries a pentacle.

Divinatory means: perfect satisfaction, happiness, ecstasy; quick intelligence, too; gold.

Reversed: evil side of wealth, misunderstanding, great wealth, too. In any event, it shows prosperity, convenient material conditions, but the advantage for the owner depends on whether the card is reversed or not.

Section 3

THE GREATER ARCANA and the MEANINGS

1. The Magician. - Talk, diplomacy, speech, subtlety, sickness, pain, loss, disaster, snares of enemies; trust, will; transversality, if male.
Reversed: Physician, Magus, dissatisfaction, mental illness.

2. The High Priestess. — Secrets, mystery, the unrevealed future; the woman interested in the transcendent, if men; the transcendent herself, if women; silence and tenacity; mystery; knowledge and the research.
Inverted: Love, spiritual or physical ardor, conceit, awareness of the air.

3. The Empress. — Fertility, effort, commitment, time; the hidden unknown; even uncertainty, doubt, ignorance. The Empress.
Reversed: light, reality, uncrowding, public rejoicing; after another reading, hesitation.

4. The Emperor. — Security, power, security, fulfillment; a great person; support, reason, belief, authority and will.
Benevolence, compassion, credit, enemies confusion, hindrance, immaturity.

5. The Hierophant. - Marriage, alliance, captivity, bondage; through another account, mercy and goodness; inspiration; the person to whom Querent resorts.

Reversed: business, good understanding, peace, over-childhood, weakness.

6. The Lovers. — Love, love, beauty, trials conquered.

Reversed: disaster, dumb designs. Another story talks of unhappy marriage and all kinds of inconsistencies.

7. The Wagon. - Succor, Providence; so war, triumph, presumption, vengeance, distress.

Reversed: Riot, quarrel, controversy, litigation, defeat.

8. Strength. - Power, energy, action, courage, magnanimity; also total success and honor.

Reversed: despotism, power abuse, weakness, discord, even disgrace, sometimes.

9. The Hermit. - Prudence, circumstance; and particularly treason, hiding, rogue, corruption.

Reversed: Overshadowing, mask, strategy, paranoia, unreasoned treatment.

10. Wealth wheel. — Destiny, wealth, achievement, upliftment, luck, congratulations.

Reversed: rise, income, superfluity.

11. Justice. — Equity, justice, integrity, executive; victory of the rule.

Reversed: Procedure, legal complications, bigotry, partiality, disproportionate severity in all agencies.

12. The Hunged Man. - Wisdom, love, discernment, decision, devotion, inspiration, divination, prophecy.

Reversed: egoism, crowd, political body.

13. Death. - For a man the loss of a benefactor; for a woman, a great deal; for a maid the failure of marriage ventures. —For a man, death, ruin, abuse,

Reversed: fatigue, sleep, lethargy, petrifaction, sleepwalking; lost hope.

14. The Temperance. - Economy, discipline, frugality, management, accommodation. Temperance.

Reversed: Churches, ideologies, denominations, priests, sometimes even the priest who marries the Querent, disunion, sad variations, competing interests.

15. The Devil. — Ravage, violence, vehemence, extraordinary efforts, strength, fatality; what is predestined, but is not evil, for that reason.

Back: bad fatality, weakness, sluggishness, blindness.

16. The Tower. - Misery, suffering, deprivation, misery, tragedy, failure, disappointment, ruin. Particularly an unforeseen catastrophe coin.

Reversed: The same in lesser degree, according to one account, also repression, prison, tyranny.

17. The Star. – Lose, robbery, deprivation and abandonment. Hope and bright prospects.

Reversed: arrogance, arrogance, powerlessness.

18. The Moon. - Hidden enemies, threat, slander, darkness, fear, frustration, occult powers, mistake.

Reversed: uncertainty, unbalance, silence, less lying and mistake.

19. Sun. - Material happiness, happiness, happiness, happiness.

Reversed: in a lesser sense the same.

20. The Last Judgment. — Change of position, reconstruction, consequence. Another account specifies total legal loss.

Reversed: weakness, pusillanimity, easiness; deliberation even, judgment, paragraph.

None. Zero. The Fool.— Folly, mania, extravagance, madness, delirium, bizarreness, mischief.

Reversed: neglect, absence, distribution, lack of care, apathy, nullity, vanity.

21. World. — Certain achievement, reward, travel, trip, emigration, flight, change of place.

Inverted: persistence, fixity, stagnation, continuity.

It is seen that except where an irresistible inference is made by the sense of the earth, what is extracted from the Trump Major by the divinatory art is at once artificial and arbitrary to the greatest degree, as I believe. But the mysteries of light are of one order, and those of imagination are of another. The assigning of a fortune-telling feature to these cards is a long story of impertinence.

22. The Fool. - Folly, mania, extravagance, intoxication, delirium, frenzy, bewrayment.

Reversed: Negligence, absence, distribution, carelessness, apathy, nullity, vanity.

Section 4

ALL THE LESSER ARCANA WANDS ADDITIONAL MEANINGS.

WANDS.

• King. – All in all favorable; can mean good marriage.

Reversed: warning to follow.

• Queen. – A good harvest that can be used in a number of ways.

Reversed: Good will to the Querent, but no chance to do it.

• Knight. – A bad card; loneliness according to some readings.

Reversed: marriage to a woman, but probably frustrated.

• Page. – Family young man looking for a young lady.

Reversed: bad news. Reversed.

• Ten. – Hardships and contradictions, if close to a good card.

• Nine. – A weak coin, generally speaking.

• Eight. – Domestic marriage disputes.

• Seven. – A dark boy.

• Six. – The servants can lose their masters' confidence; a young woman can be deceived by a relative.

Reversed: Deferred dream fulfillment.

• Five. – Financial speculation success.

Reversed: Quarrels can be converted to profit.

• Four. – Good fortune unexpected.

Reversed: A married woman will have lovely kids.

• Three. – A very good card; cooperation is going to favor business.

• Two. – A young lady could expect trivial deceptions.

• Ace. – All kinds of calamities.

Reversed: a birth sign.

CUPS.

• King. – Keep an eye on a person's ill will and on the hypocrisy that pretends to be the support.

Reversed: Loss.

• Queen. – A woman with an equivocal character sometimes denotes.

Reversed: a rich man wedding and a distinguished wedding.

• Knight. – A friend's visit, who will give the Querent an unexpected cash.

Reverse: irregularity. Reverse.

• Page. – Good prediction; also a young man in love who is unfortunate.

Reversed: all kinds of obstacles.

• Ten. – A good marriage to the male Querent and one that meets his standards.

Reversed: Sorrow; a severe war, too.

• Nine. – For positive forecasts for military men.

Reversed: Good company.

• Eight. – Fair woman's union.

Reversed: full fulfillment.

• Seven. – Equal child; thinking, design, determination, movement.

Reversed: success if the three cups are followed.

• Six. – Good memories.

Reversed: legacy to fall fast.

• Five. – Generally good; happy matrimony; even patrimony, legacies, gifts, corporate performance.

Reversed: Return of a relative who wasn't long seen.

• Four. – Antitrust.

Reversed: Presence. Reversed.

• Three. – Unforeseen progress for a military man.

Reversed: Comfort, cure, business end.

• Two.-Pleasure and enterprise as well as love; also riches and respect.

Reversed: passion. Reversed.

• Ace. – Inflexible will, unchanging rule.

Reversed: unexpected position change.

SWORDS.

• King. – A lawyer, senator, physician.

Reversed: A bad guy; also a sign to end a ruinous proceedings.

• King. – To a widow.

Reversed: a poor woman, unable to move.

• Knight. – a soldier, an armed man, a satellite, a scholarship holder, a soldier heroic action.

Reversed: Dispute with a stupid person; fight with a rival who will be conquered for a woman.

• Page. – A naked person is going to pry into the secrets of the Querent.

Reversed: Amazing news.

• Ten. – Followed by Ace and King, imprisonment; treason from friends for the girl or wife.

Reversed: victory for a soldier in battle and subsequent fortune.

• Nine. – An ecclesiastical, a priest; usually a bad omen coin.

Reversed: Solid ground for suspicious skepticism.

• Eight. – Scandal spread to a woman in her respect.

Reversed: relative's exit.

• Seven. – Dark girl; a nice card; it offers rural life after the securing of competence.

Reversed: Good advice, probably disregarded.

• Six. – The journey is sweet.

Reversed: Adverse prosecution issue.

• Five. – An assault on the Querent's wealth.

Reversed: a sign of mourning and sorrow.

• Four. – A bad card, but a qualified success can be expected from wise business administration when reversed.

Reversed: Some progress after wise administration.

• Three. – For a woman, her lover's ride.

Reversed: a meeting with someone that was corrupted by the Querent; a nun even.

• Two. – Lady's talent, powerful security for a man looking for help.

Reversed: Rogues affairs.

• Ace. – Great wealth or great suffering.

Reversed: A woman's marriage broken off through her own insensitivity.

PENTACLES.

• King. – A rather dark man, a merchant, a master, a teacher.

• Queen. – Dark wife; presents from a wealthy relative; rich and happy marriage for a young man.

Reversed: a disease.

A valuable man; useful discoveries.• Knight.

Reversed: A courageous man out of work.

• Knight. – A dark youth, a young officer or soldier, a boy.

Reversed: destruction sometimes and plundering often.

• Page. – Can mean a changing of your line of work and/or taking on more responsibility. But primarily, this is the card for students.

Reversed: Bad news, lack of goals.

• Ten. – Is house or home and derives its value from other cards.

Reversed: An ability that could be lucky or not.

• Nine. – Preview compliance with neighboring cards.

Reversed: Vain hope. Vain hope.

• Eight. – A young businessman with a Querent relationship, a dark girl.

Reversed: In a matter of money lending, the Querent is compromised.

• Seven. – Position improved for the future husband of the woman.

Reversed: Impatience, anxiety, distrust.

• Six. – One must not rely on the present.

Reversed: check on the ambition of the Querent.

• Five. – Rightly winning resources.

Reversed: Love troubles.

• Four. – To a bachelor, the lady's nice news.

Reversed: Observation, impediments.

• Three. – If a man is famous, his eldest son is famous.

Reversed: Depends on the cards. Reversed.

• Two. – Troubles are actual rather than imaginary. Bad omen, ignorance, injustice.

• Ace. – The most advantageous card of all.

Reversed: a stake of treasure-finding.

(1) those additions have few ties to the pictorial designs of the cards to which they relate, because they correspond to the most significant speculative values; (2) and further, the additional meaning very often diverges from that previously given. Both words are largely independent and are diminished, accentuated or altered and sometimes almost reversed in a series. There is little canon of criticism in such matters. I suppose that it obviously gets more unstable in proportion to the fact that all structures descend from generalities to details; and it offers more dregs and lees on the topic in the history of professional fortune telling. At the same time, the intuition-and second-view-driven divinations are little practical if they do not descend from the universal region into the particular area; but the specific meaning recorded by the previous cartomancists will not be taken into consideration

for personal assessment of the card values to the extent that this gift is present in a particular case.

This has already been intimated. The following speculative readings appear to be necessary.

Section 5

THE RECURRENCE OF CARDS IN DEALING THE NATURAL POSITION

- 4 Kings = great honor; 3 Kings = counsel; 2 Kings = no counsel.
- 4 Queens = major debate; 3 queens = women's disappointment; 2 queens = true friends.
- 4 Knights = critical matters; 3 Knights = vigorous debate; 2 Knights = intimacy.
- 4 Pages = harmful disease, 3 pages = controversy, 2 pages = worry.
- 4 Tens = condemnation; 3 Tens = new condition; 2 Tens = change.
- 4 Nines = a good friend; 3 Nines = success; 2 Nines = receipt.

• 4 Eights = reverse; 3 Eights = wedding; 2 Eights = new knowledge.

• 4 Sevens = plot; 3 Sevens = illness; 2 Sevens = news.

• 4 Sixes = plentiful; 3 Sixes = success; 2 Sixes = irritability.

• 4 Fives = regularity; 3 Fives = definition; 2 Fives = surveillance.

• 4 Fours = close to hand travel; 3 Fours = reflections; 2 Fours = insomnia.

• 4 Threes= progress; 3 Threes = unity; 2 Threes = calm.

• 4 Twos = contention; 3 Twos = safe; 2 Twos = agreement.

4 Aces = good opportunity; 3 Aces = no success; 2 Aces = trickery.

REVERSED

• 4 Kings = speed; 3 Kings = trade; 2 Kings = ventures.

• 4 Queens = bad company; 3 Queens = gluttony; 2 Queens = work.

• 4 Knights = alliance; 3 Knights = duel; 2 Knights = resistance.

• 4 Pages = poverty, 3 Pages = idleness; 2 Pages = culture.

• 4 Tens = case, happening; 3 Tens = deception; 2 Tens = reasonable expectation.

- 4 Nines = usury; 3 Nines = imprudence; 2 Nines = no money.
- 4 Eights = mistake; 3 Eights = show; 2 Eights = disaster.
- 4 Sevens = women of no repute; 3 Sevens = women of no honor. 2 Sevens = Let her go.
- 4 Sixes = care; 3 Sixes = fulfillment; 2 Sixes = decay.
- 4 Fives = order; 3 Fives = reluctance; 2 Fives = reverse.
- 4 Four = walks abroad; 3 Fours walks = discomfort; 2 Fours = controversy.
- 4 Threes = great achievement; 3 Threes= tranquility; 2 Threes= stability.
- 4 Twos = reconciliation; 3 Twos = fear; 2 Twos = mistrust.
- 4 Aces = dishonour; 3 Aces = debauchery; 2 Aces = opponents.

Section 6

THE ART OF TAROT DIVINATION

We have come to the last and practical part of this subject section which is the way of finding and receiving oracles using Tarot cards. There are various modes of action and some of them are extremely involved. I put aside those last mentioned, since people with such experience assume that the way of simplicity is the way of reality. I also set aside operations which have recently been republished in that section of The Tarot Of The Bohemians entitled "The Divine Tarot," and it can be recommended to people who would like to go beyond the limits of this manual at its proper value. First of all, I offer a short process that has been used privately in England, Scotland and Ireland for many years. I think it's not published, certainly not in relation to Tarot cards; I think it's all purposes, but I'm going, by way of variation, to add what was once known in France as Julia Orsini's Oracles.

Section 7

AN ANCIENT CELTIC DIVINATION METHOD

This method of divination is best suited for answering a specific question. The diviner first selects a card for the person or subject of the inquiry. This card is referred to as the Signifier. When he wants to find out something about himself, he takes the one that corresponds to his personal profile. A Knight should be chosen as the Significator if he or she is a man of 40 years and older, a King should be selected for any male under the age of 40, a Queen for a woman for 40 and a page for every female under the age of 40. A King should be selected.

Wands' four Court Cards are fair people, with yellow or auburn hair, white teeth and blue eyes. Cup Court Cards mean people with light brown or dark fair hair and gray or blue eyes. Those in Swords represent people with hazel or grey eyes, dark brown hair and dull teeth. Finally, in Pentacles Court cards are referred to people with very dark brown or black hair, dark eyes and salty or swarthy teeth. Nevertheless, these allocations are subject to the following reserve, which prevents them from being too traditional. You will sometimes be guided by a person's established temperament; a person who is very dark can be very robust and portray himself better by a Sword Card than by a Pentacle. On the other hand, Cups rather than the Wands should be alluded to as a rather equal subject who is indolent and lethargic.

If it is more convenient for a divination to take as a Significator the question of which investigation is to be made, the Trump or a small card that has a sense that corresponds to the issue must be chosen. Let the issue be presumed to be: will a complaint be necessary? Consider the Trump No. 11 or Justice as the Important in this situation. It applies to legal matters. But if the problem is: will I succeed in my lawsuit? The Significator must be selected as one of the Court Cards. Thereafter, consecutive divinations may be made to ascertain for each of the parties concerned the course of the process and its result.

Once the Significator has been picked, position it on the table, face upwards. Then melt the rest of the pack and cut it three times, leaving the card faces down.

Flip the top or FIRST CARD of the pack; cover the sense with it and say, "What applies to him." This card gives the power that the individual or issue usually affects, the environment in which the other currents function.

Turn the SECOND CARD up and fit the FIRST and say,' This crosses him.' This shows the essence of the obstacles. When it comes to a favorable card, the opposing forces will not be serious, or it can indicate that in a particular connection something good in itself will not be productive.

Turn the Third Card up; place it above the Point Number, and say: this crowns it. This reflects (a) the goal or ideal of Querent in the case; (b) the best that could be achieved in the circumstances but not yet actualised.

Turn the FOURTH CARD up; place it underneath the Significator, and say: it's under it. It shows the basis or the foundation of the subject, what has already become real and what the Significator has made his own.

Turn up your FIFTH CARD, place it on the sides of the indicator that you are looking at, and say: it's behind you. This gives the power that has just passed or is now fading.

N. B.-If the Significator is a trump or any small card that can not be named face to face, the Diviner will determine which side he or she will face before beginning the procedure.

Flip the SIXTH CARD onto the face of the Significator and say: this is ahead of him. This indicates the impact that will take effect and function in the near future.

The cards are now dispatched as a circle, which means that the first card is the middle of the deck.

The next four cards are turned up in succession and put on the right side of the cross above the other in a line.

The first one, or the SEVENTH CARD of the process, indicates the person or thing— that is the Significator— and shows his position or attitude under the circumstances.

The EIGHTH CARD means his house, i.e. his environment and the working tendencies therein, which affect the subject, for example his standing in life, the influence of immediate friends, etc.

The NINTH CARD offers its expectations or fears.

The TENTH is what will come, the ultimate outcome, the culmination brought about by the influences of the other cards shown in the divination.

It is on this card that the Diviner will focus in particular his intuitive ability and his memory with regard to the official divinatory meanings attached. It should be anything you have divined from other cards on the table, including the Signifier himself and involving him or herself, but lights of a higher importance than sparks of heaven if the card used for the oracle, the lecture card, was to be a Trump Major.

Now the operation has been completed, but in case the last card is questionable and no final decision is to be taken or does not seem to suggest the final conclusion of the affair, the operation could well be repeated, taking instead of the one used before the Tenth Card as the Significant in this case. The pack has to be shuffled and cut three times again and the first ten cards as before have been set out. It can provide a more detailed account of "What is to come."

If a Tenth Card should be the Court Card in any divination, it shows that the subject of the divination finally falls into the hand of a card and its end depends mainly on that person. In this case it is also useful to consider the Court Card in question as a new operation and to find out what its effect is and what the issue is about.

Good facility can be accomplished in comparatively little time by this process, making the operator's gifts always — i.e. his experience, latent or established staff — and it has a special advantage of being free of all complications.

The Significator.
1. What does it protect.
2. What is it that crosses him.
3. What makes him crown.
4. Which is below him.
5. What's inside him.
6. What ahead of him.
7. Self-sufficient.
8. His very own home.
9. His expectations or misgivings.
10. What is to come.

BIBLOGRAPHY

As I understand it is the first attempt to give in English a synoptic account of the Tarot with a given historical role, its available symbolism and — as a matter of curiosity in occultism— with its divinatory sense and modes of activity sufficiently exhibited, from the literary point of view, it is my wish, albeit modest. The following bibliographical details do not claim completeness, because I have quoted nothing which I have seen with my own eyes; but I can understand that most of my readers would be surprised about the extent of the literature that has grown up over the past 120 years, if I may call it so conventionally. Those who want to further their inquiries will find ample material in this book, but it is not a course that I am especially interested in commending, as I believe that in this place enough was said about Tarot to stand for all that preceded it. The bibliography itself is equally descriptive. I should like to add that there is a considerable catalog of cards and card player works in the British Museum, but I did not have the opportunity to consult them in any way for the purposes of this list.

I. Primitive Culture, studied and contrasted with the Modern World. By Mr. Court of Gebelin. No. Vol. Eighth, fourth, Paris, 1781.

The Jeu des Tarots posts are on pp. 365 to 410. On the plates at the end of each suit are the Trump Major and the Ases. These are useful as card signals at the end of the 18th century. They possibly circulated in the south of France at that point, as it is said that at that time in Paris they were virtually unknown. I have addressed the papers ' claims in the body of the present work. Their work was reasonably tolerable for its mazy period; however, that French occult writers still suffer and indeed embrace them without question is the most compelling evidence that one can have to have the skills of French authors to deal with any issue of historical research.

II. The Oeuvre of Etteilla. The seventh complexities of the Hermetic philosophical work; manner of recreating themselves with the game of charts, called Tarot; Fragments on the high sciences; Philosophy of the high sciences; Game of the Tarot, or the book of Thoth; Theoretical and Practical Lection of the book of the Thoth— all published between 1783 and 1787.

These are extremely rare and frankly included in the works of colportage of their own time. We have the most interest about stuff in and without the main problem, lucubrations about creativity, sorcery, astrology, talismans, dreams, etc. I have also addressed the views of the author on the Tarot and its position in modern history in the article. He found it to be a work of speaking hieroglyphics, but it was not easy to translate. But he accomplished the task— that is, in his own view.

III. An investigation into the ancient Greek game that Palamedes was supposed to have invented. London: 4to, 1801. (By James Christie.)

I list this series of interesting theses because the Tarot authors quoted them. This aims at creating a close link between early ancient and modern chess games. The discovery credited to Palamedes before the Siege of Troy is suggested to be recognized in China since ancient times. The work does not refer to cards of any kind.

IV. Investigation into play card culture. By Weller Singer. By Samuel Weller Singer. Fourth, London, 1816.

The Tarot may well be of Eastern origin and high antiquity but the rest of the theory of the Court of Gebelin is baseless and unclear. Cards were popular in Europe before the Egyptians appeared. The thesis has plenty of interesting details and the appendices are useful, but the Tarot takes very little part in the text and the time for a substantive critique of its arguments is too early. Excellent reproductions of early specimen designs are available. The Court de Gebelin is also given extensively.

V. Playing Card Figures and Speculations. Through W. A. Chatto. London, 8vo, 1848.

The author suggested that the Major Trumps and the number cards were once distinct but eventually merged. The earliest Tarot card examples are not older than 1440. Nevertheless, the arguments and the volume value have been defined adequately in the text.

VI. Playing Cards and Cartomancie. By D. R. P. Boiteau of Ambly. France, Paris, 4th, 1854.

There are some interesting examples of the early Tarot cards which are said to have Eastern roots, but not Egypt. The early association of gypsies is verified, but there is no proof. The cards were issued by gipsies from India, where they were intended to show "the unknown divinity," rather than to serve profane entertainment.

VII. Dogma and Practice of Black Magic. By Eliphas Levi, 2 flights., demy 8vo, Paris, 1854.

This is Alphonse Louis Constant's first publication on occult philosophy and is also his magnum opus. It is built on the key keys of the Tarot in both volumes and was therefore understood as a type of development of their implications as presented in the author's mind. To complete the work in this monograph, I just need to add that the transmutations portion of the second volume includes what is referred to as the Key of Thoth. This inner circle shows a triple Tau with a hexagram that joins the bases, and the As of Cups is below. The letters TARO are inside the external circle and all about this figure are grouped the cards of the four living creatures, of the walls ace, of the sword ace, the Shin letter and a magician's candle, which, as Levi says, are identical with the lights of the Black Evocations and Pacts Gothic Circle. The Triple Tau can be taken as the As of the Pentacles. The only Tarot card in the volumes is the Chariot drawn by two sphinxes, which was followed in the later days. These are the traditional mystic students who view the work as a kind of commentary on the Trumps World, while those who ignore it will just have the agony of fools.

VIII. The Romans. By J. A. Vaillant. Paris, Paris, 1857. The author tells us how he met the cards, but he's in an anecdote segment. The Tarot is Enoch's sidereal text, based on Athor's astral wheel. There a summary of the Trump Major, obviously considered a heirloom brought from Indo-Tartary gipsies. I think that the publications of Lévi's Dogme et Rituel have made a huge impact on him, and while in this most important work of the writer, the anecdote I have described is basically his only Tarot reference, in a later publication he appears to have gone much further— Clef Magiques de la Fiction et du Fait, but I could not or do not think from the records.

IX. History of Magic. Through Eliphas Levi. Paris, 1860. 8vo, 1860.

In this brilliant work, which will soon be available within English, the references to the Tarot are few. It gives the 21st Trump Major, often referred to as the Universe or World, as Yinx Pantomorph — a standing figure carrying the Isis crown. This was repeated in Le Tarot Divinatoire by Papus. The writer explains that the existing Tarot came down to us through the Jews, but he was somehow handled by the Gipsies, who brought it with them when they entered France at the beginning of the 15th century. Vaillant is the authority here.

X. The Secret to the Great Mysteries. By Eliphas Levi, Paris, 8vo, 1861.

The frontispiece of this work reflects William Postel's absolute key to the supernatural sciences, completed by the artist. It is reproduced in The Tarot Of The Bohemians and, as elsewhere, I explained in the preface I prefixed to this that Postel never made a hieroglyphic key. The Tarot is the sacred alphabet, referred diversely to Enoch, Thoth, Cadmus and Palamedes by Eliphas Lévi. This consists of pure concepts connected to numbers and signs. The latter is discussed in a broad way as far as number 19 is concerned, the series being construed as the keys of occult theology. The other three numbers that complete the Hebrew alphabet are called the Nature Keys. The Tarot is said to be the original of Chess, as it also belongs to the Royal Goose Game. This book contains the fictional reconstruction of the 10th Trump Major by the author, which shows Egyptian figures on the Wheel of Fortune.

XI. The Red Man of Tuileries. By Fr. Christian. Fcap. Fcap. France, 1863, 8vo.

The work is unique, sought after and once highly valued in France; but Dr. Papus has awakened to the fact that it is of slender interest and can broaden the assertion. However, it is interesting that the author's first meditations are contained on the Tarot. He became Lévi's follower and imitator. In his current work he comments on the Trump Major and then on the designs and meanings of the whole Minor Arcana. There are many curious attributions to astrology. The work does not appear to name the Tarot. A later Histoire de la Magie reproduces and expands the Trump Major account given herein.

XII. Playing Card History. Via E. S. Taylor. Cr. Cr. 8vo. 8vo. London, 1865. London.
This has been posthumously published and is essentially a Boiteau translation. That is why it calls for little comment on my part. The belief is that cards were smuggled from India by gypsies. There are also references to the so-called Chinese Tarot, which the Court of Gebelin described.

XIII. Source of Playing Cards. Via Romain Merlin. Paris, Paris, 4th, 1869.
Except in the imagination of Court de Gebelin, there is no reason for the Egyptian roots of the Tarot. Otherwise I have mentioned that the writer disposes of the gypsy hypothesis to his personal satisfaction, and that he does the same as regards the supposed connection to India; he says that in Europe cards were known before communication with that world was generally opened in 1494. But if the gipsies were already a Pariah tribe living in the West and if the

cards were part of your luggage, then there is nothing in this conflict. The whole thing is basically a question of conjecture.

XIV. The Platonist. The Platonist. Vol. Vol. II, 126-8. II. Published 1884-5 in St. Louis, Mo., U.S.A. Royal 4th. 4th.

This publication, of which many admirers of an unselfish and hard work must have regretted its suspension, included an anonymous essay by a writer with theosophical instincts and great pretensions for information on the Tarot. However, it has strong titles of negligence on its own basis and is indeed a ludicrous achievement. The Latin Rota= wheel, transposed, is Tarot. The system was invented in India at a distant time, possibly— the author is unclear— about B. C. 300. 300. The Fool is the underlying chaos. The Tarot is now in use by Rosicrucians, but despite the suggestion it might have come down to them in the early 17th century from their German parents and despite the source in India, the 22 keys on the walls of Egyptian temples were dedicated to the mysteries of the Initiation. Some of this scrap comes from P. Christian but the following assertion, I believe, is unique to the author: "Followers know that there should be 22 mystical keys, that would make a total number of 100." Persons reaching a certain stage of lightness have to provide only blank pasteboards with the number they need, and the missing designs are furnished with higher intelligences. Meanwhile, America awaits the fulfillment of the final prophecy that few have produced so far in that country "to read beautifully... in the great and divine work of sybilline Taro." Perhaps the cards that accompany the current volume can give a chance and a boost!

XV. The Yoke of Naips. By Joseph Brunet and Bellet. Cr. Cr. Eighteenth, Barcelona, 1886.

The author quotes E in respect to the vision of Egyptian origin. Garth Wilkinson's etiquette and Egyptian customs at least prove that the cards in the ancient cities of the Delta are unknown. Following the chief authorities, the history of the subject is drawn up, without regard to exponents of occult colleges. The key is Chatto. There are some very interesting facts about card ban in Spain, and the appendices include a number of important documents, one of which reveals that St. Bernardin from Sienna preached against games in general, and cards in particular, in 1423. There are depictions of the rude Tarots, including a strange description of a phoenix of a cup of cups and of a Queen of cups, whose vessel produces a fruit.

XVI. The Tarot: its supernatural sense, the use of luck, and the play form. Via S.L. MacGregor Mathers. Sq. Sq. Friday, London, 1888.

This booklet was intended to accompany a variety of Tarot cards, and the new shipments from abroad have been imported for this purpose. The author or the only personal opinion expressed here notes that the Trump Major cards are hieroglyphic and correspond to the mystical nature of the Hebrew alphabet. Here the authority is Lévi, from whom also the short symbolism assigned to the 22 Keys is derived. The divinatory significances follow, and then the operating modes. It is just a sketch written pretentiously and in all respects it is negligible.

XVII. Methodical Agreement of Occult Studies. By Papus. By Papus. Paris, 8vo, 1891.

This work reproduces the Tarot rectified which Oswald Wirth has published after the indications of Eliphas Lévi, which—it can be mentioned—extends to almost 1,100 pages. There is a section on the gypsies that are regarded through the cards as importers of esoteric tradition to Europe. The Tarot is a blend of numbers and concepts that fit the Hebrew alphabet. Sadly, countless typographical mistakes render the Hebrew quotes almost unintelligible.

XVIII. Eliphas Levi: The Book of Splendors. Paris, Paris, 1894.
(a) the Tarot contains a fourfold explanation of numbers 1 to 10 in several of the four cards; (b) cards which we only have now in the forme of cards were first medals then become talismans; (c) the Tarot is the hieroglyphic book of the Thirty-two Courses of the Theosophy of Kabalism and its summation is I have dealt with the historical value of these pretensions in the text.

XIX. Solomon's Magic Keys and Clavicles. By Eliphas Levi. Sq. Sq. Paris, 12mo, 1895.
In 1860, with their primitive pureté, the keys concerned are said to have been restored by hieroglyphic signs and numbers, without any admixture of Samaritan or Egyptian pictures. There are rude sketches of the Hebrew letters attributed to the Trump Major with meanings, most of which can be found by the same writer in other works. There are also combinations of the letters which enter the Divine name; the court cards of the Lesser Arcana

are assigned to these combinations. Some mystical talismans have Tarot attributions in fine; the Ace of Clubs refers to the First Law, the Deus Absconditus. The little book was published at a high price and was to be reserved for adherents or those on the road of obedience, but it is truly worthless— symbolically or not.

XX. The XXII Hermetic Lames of Divinatory Tarot. Via R. Falconnier. Paris, Paris, 1896.
It means "fixed star," which in turn signifies immutable tradition, theosophical synthesis, the symbolism of original dogma, etc. The word tarot is derived from Sanskrit. Graven on golden plates, Hermes Trismegistus ' designs were used and their mysteries revealed only in Isis ' highest priesthood. Therefore, it is unnecessary to say that the Tarot comes from Egypt and the work of M. Falconnier has re-constructed its primitive form, which he does in terms of its monuments — that is, he sketches the trumps main designs in the imitation of Egyptian sculpture after the fashion of Eliphas Lévi. This creation was praised by French occultists as the ideal Tarot, but the same was said of Oswald Wirth's designs which are entirely unlike Egyptian. To be honest, such foolishness could be expected to be as

much from the Sanctuary of the Comédie-Française, to which the author belongs and should be reserved for it.

XXI. Sanctum Regnum's Divine Ritual, represented by the Trump Tarot. MSS translated. Translated. Eliphas Lévi's and W's edited. Fcap, M.B. Wynn Westcott, 8vo, London, 1896.

It must be said that this memorial's interest lies more in its existence than in its intrinsic importance. There is some sort of informal comment on the Trump Major, or rather there are considerations that the French author presumably thought of. For instance, the card called Fortitude is a way of exploring the will as a secret of power. The Hanged Man is said to be the end of the Great Work. Death implies a diatribe to Necromancy and Goëtia; but such fantasies do not exist in "the Sanctum Regnum." Temperance creates only a few empty places, and the Devil, who is a blind force, is an opportunity to repeat much that has already been said in Lévi's earlier work. The Tower is the betrayal of the Great Arcanum, and it was this that caused Samael's sword to spread over the Garden of Delight. Among the plates is a Gnosis monogram which is also the Tarot monogram. The writer carefully inserted details on the Trump Cards

from Lévi's early works and P's remarks. Christian.
Christian.

XXII. How to become an alchemist. By F. Jolivet of
Castellot. Sq. Sq. Paris, 1897, 8vo.
This is the description of the Alchemical Tarot,
which—with all my reverence for developments and
technologies —seems to be extremely imaginative;
but Etteilla was admired in this way and it could be
worth tabulating analogies of those weird dreams if
it should ever be possible to create a Key Major
instead of the present Key Minor. It shall be enough
for now to say that a schedule is issued to Trump
Major, with alchemical correspondences that seem
to symbolize desirable power by the Juggler or
Magician; the High Priestess is inert matter, which
nothing is more false; the Papal is the Quintessence,
which — if he only knew Shakespeare — would
tempt the present successor of St. Petite If this
encourages my readers, they can also note, if these
are laid down for the purpose, that the details of
different chemical combinations can be developed
via the Lesser Arcana. The King of Walls= gold; the
pages or the knaves are animal substances; the King
of the Cups= silver; etc.

XXIII. The Great Arcane, or revealed occultism. By Eliphas Levi. London, Paris, 1898.

After many years and the extensive experience of occultism with all of his questions, the author reduces his message to one simple solution in this book. Of course I just talk about the Tarot: he claims that Etteilla's cards create a kind of hypnotism in the seer who thus divines. The madness of the psychic is read in the madness of the querant. Unless he counseled integrity, he would lose his clients. I've written serious criticisms about occult arts and science, but that is surprising from one of their past professors, and I think that the psychic sometimes is psychic and sees as such.

XXIV. The Serpent of Genesis — Book II; The Key to Black Magic. By Stanislas of Guaita. London, Paris, 1902.

This is a vast commentary on the Trump Major's second seventh. Justice means equilibrium and its agent; the Hermit is characteristic of the mysteries of solitude; the wheel of fortune is the circus of becoming or achieving; strength means the force of will; hanged man is mystical slavery that speaks volumes for the blurry and twisted dream of this illusion by the occultism; death, of course, is what its name means, but with reversion. There's more of the same thing in the first book, I believe, but this is a specimen. The death of Stanislas de Guaita brought his scheme of analysis of Tarot Trumps to an end, but the connection is vague and the actual references can be reduced to a few lines.

XXV. Le Tarot: Historical overview. By. By. J. J. Bourgeat. Bourgeat. Sq. Sq. Paris, 12mo, 1906.
The creator illustrated his work with purely fictional creations, such as the Wheel of Fortune, Death and the Devil. We are irrelevant to symbolism. The Tarot is said to have come from India, where it went to Egypt. P. Christian, Eliphas Levi, and J. A. In support of comments and opinions, Vaillant is quoted. The mode of divination is clearly and thoroughly established.

CPSIA information can be obtained
at www.ICGtesting.com
Printed in the USA
LVHW080308130421
684250LV00022B/2339